Reflections on Life

By the same Author

MAN THE UNKNOWN

PRAYER

VOYAGE TO LOURDES

Alexis Carrel

Reflections on Life

Translated from the French
by Antonia White

Hawthorn Books, Inc.

New York

SECOND PRINTING
November, 1953

Contents

Introduction

The spirit bloweth where it listeth. It is folly for anyone not animated by its breath to express his thoughts in public; it is liable to result in total misunderstanding between this presumptuous person and those whom he addresses. Nevertheless, I am going to attempt to explain to men of good will the circumstances which induced Carrel to write this book.

When France was invaded, he was in New York where he had been sent on a government mission. Nothing forced him to return; he was among his dearest friends, those who understood his thought and admired his work.

Nevertheless, as in 1914, he felt the call of his country as imperative; he sacrificed everything to it and came back.

He wanted to find out for himself what the people needed, and to remedy, with all the knowledge at his command, the defects he perceived in the young people of France, but which distance prevented him from judging accurately.

No sooner had he arrived than he became aware of the great moral, physical and physiological confusion which,

7

combined with undernourishment, was undermining a section of the people and threatening their ruin.

After a fierce inner struggle, his mind was made up. He would not return, even temporarily, to America where it would have been easy for him to carry on with the plans for his final work. That work was the child of his thought and, thanks to the disciples whom he would have trained, should have survived him and achieved the aim he had set himself.

For him, indeed, the "science of man" differed at all points from the classical sciences: each of which only envisaged one particular aspect of the human being and artificially dissected him in order to study only his component parts. Carrel's conception tended toward a total synthesis which would use all the available material and integrate it into a higher knowledge. Man was to be apprehended as a whole, in the totality of his physiological, mental and spiritual functions.

He would have wished to confide this work to a small group of men of the highest caliber who would be set apart from the ordinary contingencies of life. They would live in an atmosphere of calm which would allow them to concentrate themselves into a genuine "collective brain." This would have been the converging point of all the work put at his disposal by a method which Carrel described as "collective thought."

As a Frenchman, it was in France that he believed he ought to attempt the realization of this plan. The French Foundation for the Study of Human Problems was the preliminary sketch. With the help of young people whom he wished to train according to his methods and without taking into account the obstacles and the terrible difficulties he met at every step, he undertook this superhuman task which drove him to his death.

Although extremely depressed by the fact of the Occupation and, like all his compatriots, deprived of all comforts and weakened by undernourishment, he set himself resolutely to work. He would work with his legs wrapped in a blanket in an effort to fight the cold which he feared so much.

He hoped to live some years more in order to bring the task, whose outlines he could clearly distinguish, to fruition. God did not permit it. In spite of the moral support of friends who remained faithful to the end and who surrounded him with sincere affection, his heart was too exhausted. Mortally wounded by the calumnies of certain envious people, it could not resist the malice of those who caused his death.

He accepted it with full knowledge and with the serenity of a Christian. In his tireless activity, he had resolved to pass on his knowledge to his "neighbor" before he died. He would have called this book *The Conduct of Life.*

Had he lived a few months longer, this book, begun before the war and written entirely by his own hand, would have been differently presented. It is composed of material assembled by him and destined to be sifted, polished and completed before being set out in that precise and living language of which he had the secret.

In such conditions, why let this work appear? For five years I debated the question with myself and others. I was overwhelmed with contradictory advice. But my own conclusion is that I have no right to keep his last counsels only for my personal comfort.

These last reflections, though incomplete, are addressed above all to those who wish to continue and develop the ideas sketched in these chapters. They will understand that the premature death of Alexis Carrel prevented him from giving this "Testament" the finish to which he had accustomed us.

My hope resides in the young who were the object of his

preoccupation and of his affection. Some among them will feel the truth contained in these pages, unfinished as they are.

They will help them in difficult times to push open those doors behind which a useful, perhaps even a happy, life awaits them. One part of his aim will have been achieved.

In this hope, I launch his "ship" on the wide ocean, hoping that she will find a good harbor though the pilot is no longer at her helm.

"*A Dieu vat . . .*"

ANNE CARREL

Preface

The great question today is how to improve both the mental and organic state of civilized humanity; that is to say, how to work for the development of beings superior to any who have hitherto inhabited the earth. This enterprise is necessary because our intelligence has not increased at the same rate as the complexity of the problems to be solved. Thus we are on the downward path. Modern society has been preoccupied with material values. It has neglected fundamental human problems which are both material and spiritual. Not only has it not brought us happiness but it has shown itself incapable of preventing our deterioration. The conquest of health is not enough. We must also bring about in every individual the finest development of his hereditary power and of his personality, for the quality of life is more important than life itself.

We must therefore find the means of artificially producing in every man activities which, while increasing his capacity to adapt himself to the social and cosmic world, will also stimulate his mental development. These activities manifest themselves especially in moral sense, judgment, robustness of spirit and resistance to folly. They spring from intelligence and intuition. But, to be really useful, character and intelligence demand as substratum a balanced nervous system, organic strength and natural immunity to disease.

During growth, body and mind possess great plasticity. This plasticity permits them to obey the influence of all the factors in their environment. Innumerable observations have shown that climate, profession, diet, athletics, certain intellectual and moral disciplines, etc., make a deep imprint on the personality. Even variations of one single condition of development, such as diet, are enough to produce great changes in animals. In the course of experiments made at the Rockefeller Institute in New York the size of pure-bred mice was increased or reduced at will. In one group, the average weight of the young at one month old went down to just over 6 grams while, in another group, it reached over 11 grams. The length of life proved to be equally modifiable. In one large group, given an excellent diet, 9 per cent of the mice lived more than twenty months. In another group, given the same food two days a week, the number of mice who lived longer than twenty months rose to 60 per cent. The mortality of the young before weaning was also influenced by the diet of the mothers and went down from 52 per cent to 19 per cent. Changes in diet modified the natural resistance to pneumonia. As many as 52 per cent of the mice which made up one of the groups died of pneumonia. An improvement in the regime lowered the mortality to 32 per cent, another modification to 14 per cent. The addition of a certain chemical substance completely suppressed the disease. But, in this last group, as many as 83 per cent of the mice died of tumor of the liver, at a later age. More subtle characteristics appeared. In one group which for several years received a diet excellent in quality but insufficient in quantity, the size became smaller while the intelligence markedly increased. On the contrary, both intelligence and size diminished in a group which was given sea water with its food.

These observations show the great fluidity possessed by the living organism. It is, therefore, not unreasonable to try to obtain, by a wise use of physical, chemical and physiological factors, a spiritual improvement of the human being.

The formation of body and mind depends on the chemical, physical and psychological conditions of the environment and on physiological habits. The effects of these conditions and these habits on the whole make-up of the individual ought to be exactly studied with reference to all activities of body and mind.

A. *Effects of Chemical Factors.*—Thanks to the science of nutrition, we know how to feed children so that they will grow tall and strong and their death rate will be extremely low. But this science has not taught us how to give them a robust nervous system, a balanced disposition, courage, moral sense and intelligence, nor how to protect them against mental degeneration. This problem concerns the future of millions of children. It is urgent, therefore, to begin to study it. It can be approached by three convergent methods.

The first will consist in repeating the experiments made on mice and rats on a very large group of extremely intelligent and pure-bred dogs. With the help of psychological and chemical tests, it would be possible to measure the effect of different diets and of certain chemical substances on the mental and organic state of these animals.

As dogs become adult in one year, many results would be rapidly obtained. But others, such as the effects of feeding on degenerative diseases and on longevity, would appear much more slowly. One would have to perform these experiments over a period of something like twenty-five years.

The second method would include the examination, from the point of view of alimentary regimes, of human groups which have not yet been standardized and also of groups of men or animals who have been naturally isolated in particular conditions of existence. Some retrospective studies would probably be possible. Furthermore, one would submit to a critical examination the regimes approved by the medical body and those alimentary superstitions which have important results on the psychological and organic stage of large groups of individuals.

The third method would be experimental. It would consist in applying the data we already possesss, and those which will be shortly acquired, to groups of children in Europe, America and Africa. This experiment would last over a hundred years.

B. *Effects of Physical Factors.*—Civilization tends to suppress natural climate. By protecting men against inclemencies of weather and by submitting them to new physical conditions in houses, offices and factories, it has created artificial climates. It is necessary, therefore, to study the influence of heat, damp, uniformity of temperature, wind, dust, fields of electricity, gases, noise, etc., on the organic, nervous and psychological state. This problem will be approached by the same methods as the preceding one. The results obtained will be valuable indications for the construction of houses and towns and for general habits of life.

C. *Effects of Physiological Habits.*—The way in which each individual uses the factors of his environment depends to a great extent on his physiological habits. These habits vary according to the organic and mental type. This is why we ought to study in individuals of different types such things as the effect of the amount of sleep, of the frequency and abundance of meals, of manual work, physical exercises, inclement weather, prolonged effort, etc.

The only aim of these three examples is to indicate how this question of the improvement of the individual can be approached in a concrete way. But they are far from exhausting the subject. For example, it has been possible to make organs separated from the body go on living in an apparatus invented by Lindbergh. This is an ideal method for studying the nutrition of the glands. The discovery of the food needed by an organ may lead to a method of stimulating its activity when this diminishes. It would be far more valuable to reestablish the glandular function in this way than to inject patients with hormones. In the spiritual domain, we are completely ignorant of the conditions of development of certain nonintellectual activities such as moral sense, esthetic sense and intuition. Nevertheless, we know that intuition is one of the essential factors in a man's superiority. This quality probably belongs to the same order as clairvoyance and telepathy. It would therefore be of great practical interest to begin a scientific study of these normal phenomena.

In the same way, we ought to try to produce a certain number of individuals above the mental stature which we observe in the best. This research could be made on dogs, by submitting them to combinations of certain environmental factors. In less than two years, results would already be appearing. The creation of an elite is of capital importance. No modern man has sufficient intelligence and courage to attack the great problems of civilization. It would be extremely important to place children who already have a good heredity in a physical, chemical and psychological environment carefully adapted to their types. One might thus obtain very highly gifted individuals. Society has need of supermen now that it is no longer capable of directing itself and Western civilization is shaken to its foundations.

To obtain this result, there is no need for imposing buildings nor for great sums of money nor for a bureaucratic scheme. All that is needed is small, independent, self-administering units. The organization of a new unit or the disorganization of an old one would have no effect on the others. Cheap and simple buildings could be put up, designed specifically to deal with a given problem and with no concern for architectural beauty. The apparatus of this research center would be the cerebral matter of a small group of men devoted to the complex problem whose solution would be the aim of the enterprise. The essential function of this group would be to guide the researches in the desired direction and to assure their continuity over a long period of time. One must not forget that certain experiments made on human beings need be prolonged over more than a hundred years. The synthetic character of this work demands that its direction should never fall into the hands of specialists in biology, psychology or any other science. Only men of very comprehensive intelligence, free from all doctrine or prejudice, are capable of envisaging physiological and mental problems from a truly human point of view. Undoubtedly, specialists will be needed to work in conjunction with these men. Happily there are plenty of excellent specialists; it is only the nonspecialized minds with a synthetic outlook which are rare. Nevertheless, their role in the direction of a research center is of prime importance. We must not forget that the Kaiser Wilhelm Institute developed admirably under a theologian of wide intelligence, Adolph von Harneck. The success of the Rockefeller Institute is due to Simon Flexner who abandoned his own researches to interest himself in all sciences. Recently the Rockefeller Foundation has judged it opportune to put at its head, not a scientist but a lawyer whose mind is capable of grasping the most varied subjects. It is men of this intellectual type who will be the soul of the new research center.

This institution will in no way be a rival to the great research institutes, such as the Rockefeller Institute, the Pasteur Institute and the Kaiser Wilhelm Institute, nor to any other institution. Its work will be complementary to theirs and have an entirely different aim. This aim will be the synthetic study of organisms endowed with intelligence, not the separate analysis of physiological or psychological processes toward which the efforts of all the biological institutes are directed. Furthermore, it will eventually apply this synthetic knowledge and the fragmentary data we already possess, not to the sick but to the improvement of normal individuals. Instead of encouraging the survival of the unfit and the defective, we must help the strong; only the elite makes the progress of the masses possible. Hitherto, no scientific institute has devoted itself to the formation of men of superior quality. For this reason, it is urgent to found an organization capable of undertaking this work.

This organization will be entirely concerned with individuals belonging to the races who produced the Western civilization to which they belong. Its center will be in Europe but its units may be situated in any part of the world where it is desirable or expedient to carry out certain investigations.

Reflections on Life

CHAPTER ONE

Disobedience to the Rules of Life

<table>
<tr><td>1</td><td>The Revolt against Ancestral Rules of Behavior.—Its History.—Liberation from the Constraints Imposed by the Cosmic Environment and Christian Morality. Abandonment of all Discipline: Individual, Social and Racial.</td></tr>
</table>

Everyone feels the desire to live according to his own fancy. This desire is innate in man, but, in democratic nations, it becomes so peculiarly inflamed that it ends by acquiring a positively morbid intensity. It was the philosophers of the Century of Enlightenment who enthroned this blind cult of liberty in Europe and America. In the name of reason, they heaped ridicule on the traditional disciplines, thus rendering every kind of constraint odious or absurd. Then began the final period of the struggle against the rules of conduct which our ancestors accepted; rules which owed their origin to the experience humanity had acquired over thousands of years and to the moral teaching of the Gospels.

To be accurate, our emancipation began over four hundred years ago. Nevertheless, in spite of the immense effort of the eighteenth century, its achievement is hardly in sight today, for its ultimate success depends on the progress of scientific knowledge. To enjoy total liberty, we have not merely to free ourselves from old ideas but to obtain mastery over the material world. This mastery can only come about through science. But science had a long and difficult childhood and its maturity barely dates back to yesterday. This is why we have delayed so long in proclaiming our independence of ancestral modes of life and thought.

This revolt has a long history. It began during the Renaissance. In that period there occurred an apparently insignificant event. Copernicus demonstrated that the earth is merely a satellite of the sun. Immediately, the world of Ptolemy crumbled; the earth was shorn of its proud pre-eminence as center of the universe. The Church was alarmed, with good reason, but in vain. The trial of Galileo emphasized still further the importance of this revolution. The world of Aristotle, of St. Thomas Aquinas, of Dante, ceased to exist; that logical, complete, comfortable world where man only sojourned on earth to prepare himself for a future life; where heaven and hell were within our reach.

At the same time, earth as well as heaven acquired a disquieting vastness. Marco Polo had already revealed to the West the fabulous immensity of Asia. The New World had opened up before Christopher Columbus; Vasco da Gama had discovered the route to the Indies. There was an amazing outburst of adventurers, conquerors, pioneers and apostles. The wealth of Europe accumulated prodigiously and, with it, the desire to know and master the material world. The era of Science had begun. A few years before the appearance of Machiavelli, Copernicus and Luther, Gutenberg had discovered printing. New ideas could thus be rapidly diffused. Side by side with the affirmations of philosophy and religion came the certainty which results from the systematic observation of phenomena. The clarity of scientific concepts, arrived at by the intellect alone, challenged the light of faith. God, with His angels and His saints, began to seem far away. Then began the corrosion of the framework which for so long had kept our medieval ancestors in a hitherto unparalleled state of spiritual and social stability. Luther's attacks had severely shaken the authority of the Church over individuals and peoples. Christendom was divided; the nations of Europe were beginning to take shape. Thus was sown the seed which, after centuries of incubation, was to bring about war between all the nations of the world and to threaten universal chaos.

By a very similar process, the seeds of division were sown in the core of the individual conscience. The conflict of faith, philosophy and science was an apple of discord in the soul of Western man. There was no longer an inflexible rule of behavior and moral discipline grew slack. The beauty of art and poetry was preferred to the beauty of virtue. The will, ceasing to aspire toward another world, confined itself to acquiring the goods of this one. As Machiavelli had boldly proclaimed, the end of human existence is not God, but profit. Economic forces had begun their ascent toward supreme power.

Nevertheless, since Europe was deeply saturated with Christianity, the old customs did not disintegrate at once or completely. The people had not forgotten that it was they who had built the Gothic cathedrals. The spire which rose above the village was a true symbol of the aspiration of the human community toward the divine. Reason needed many centuries before it could obscure and darken faith. Moreover, the hard struggle for existence forbade the jettisoning of rules of conduct necessary for the survival of the race. Technology perfected itself only by very slow degrees. Nevertheless, it tended more and more to creat conditions which made it possible for man to behave according to his fancy. At the same time, the smoldering quarrel between philosophy and science broke into fiercer flame. In the domain of inert matter, science triumphed; it engendered the race of machines and made us masters of the earth. But, in the domain of the human, that is to say of individual and social conduct, it was vanquished. The logical constructions of the mind took precedence over the data of observation and experience. Ideologies were preferred to scientific concepts or to religious morality. Pascal was abandoned in favor of Descartes; the clarity of an idea was supposed to be the touchstone of its truth. Henceforth, any logical ideology, any fantasy of the intellect, appeared worthy to serve as a base for human behavior, provided only it was rational. No one understood that, if it is to endure, a civilization must be built, not on philosophical principles but on scientific concepts of the human being and his environment.

The tendencies symbolized by Machiavelli, Luther and Galileo tunneled obscurely in men's minds for several decades. It was not till the eighteenth century that they emerged into daylight. Then, under the influence of Voltaire and the Encyclopedists, they launched themselves openly. It was in the name of those symbols that the United States proclaimed their independence. It was recognized that the power of the rulers depended on the consent of the ruled and that each individual was free to pursue happiness in his own way.

At the same time, the Industrial Revolution was rapidly spreading throughout England. Adam Smith loudly proclaimed the new religion in his book *The Wealth of Nations*. The businessman became a kind of public benefactor. By a curious process of juggling, the unlimited freedom of a few to acquire wealth was considered as the condition of happiness for all.

It was in this period, too, that Lavoisier laid the foundations of modern chemistry. It was the dawn of liberty, prosperity and the triumph of science. The future opened bright with promise.

The French Revolution broke out. The aristocrat was replaced by the bourgeois and military feudalism by capitalism. Economic liberalism began its rise, a rise which was to be one long triumphal progress from Waterloo to the first world war. That same period saw science working a continuous transformation of modes of life and thought. On the other hand, religion proved itself incapable of resisting the attacks of rationalism. Under the influence of inextricably interwoven factors such as dechristianization, the development of technology, the increase of wealth and material comfort, the motorcar, the cinema and the radio, the moral tone of society became lower and lower. The moment had come for civilized people to throw overboard the last relics of the old ancestral disciplines.

In the soothing softness of the modern world, the mass of traditional rules which gave consistency to life broke up as the frozen surface of a stream breaks up in spring. This breaking up is as characteristic of the individual as it is of the family and of society. We are freed from the hard labor imposed on our muscles, our organs, our nervous systems and our minds by the necessity of forcing the earth to yield our daily bread, by the threat of famine, by the difficulty of communications through forest, marsh and mountain. We no longer have to keep up an incessant struggle against heat, cold, drought, wind, rain and snow. We no longer dread the long winter nights or isolation in the inaccessible depths of the country. Science has miraculously taken the edge off the bitter struggle for everyday life. We are fed, clothed, sheltered, transported and even educated by the work of machines. Thanks to the progress of technology, the greater part of the restraints imposed on us by the cosmos have disappeared and, along with them, the creative personal effort which those restraints demanded.

We have abandoned the struggle against ourselves as eagerly as that against our environment. Without troubling to ask ourselves whether the traditional rules were not necessary for the success of individual and collective life, we have emancipated ourselves from all moral discipline. The frontiers of good and evil have vanished in a mist of ideologies, whims and appetites. In the ancient community as in the modern, morality was bound up with religion. In Greece, when the Sophists destroyed belief in the gods of Olympus and the fear they inspired, each man behaved according to his own fancy. The moral laws which had formed the soul of Western civilization from its cradle were founded on belief in a future life, on divine revelation, on the dogmas of the Church and on the love of Christ. Naturally these did not survive the disappearance of faith.

As soon as we renounced the precepts of the Gospel, we renounced all interior discipline. The new generation is not even aware that such a discipline ever existed. Temperance, honor, truthfulness, responsibility, purity, self-mastery, love of one's neighbor, heroism are outworn expressions; meaningless words which provoke nothing but a contemptuous smile from the young. Religious beliefs, when they are sincere, inspire the kind of respect accorded to rare objects in a museum. Admittedly, in the groups which have remained Catholic, people still speak readily of charity, justice and truth. But, apart from a faithful few, no one applies these principles to ordinary life. For modern man, the only rule of conduct is his own good pleasure. Everyone is enclosed in his own egoism like the crab in its shell and, again like the crab, seeks to devour his neighbor. Elementary social relations have changed profoundly; everywhere, division reigns. Marriage has ceased to be a permanent bond between man and woman. Both the material and the psychological conditions of modern existence have created a propitious climate for the breaking up of family life. Children are now considered a nuisance, if not a calamity. This is the final result of having abandoned those rules which, in the past, Western man had the courage and wisdom to impose on his individual and social conduct.

2 | *Organization of Society according to Philosophical Speculations.—Misunderstanding of Scientific Concepts.—Liberalism and Marxism.—The Triumph of Ideologies.*

It would have been possible for us to use our acquired freedom to establish a solid base for our communal existence. We have not, however, done so. The behavior of men of our time must therefore be a subject of extreme astonishment to future generations. It is, in fact, strange that a society as alert as our own to the power of scientific methods and ideas should not have used these methods to organize its own life. Science has given us the mastery over almost everything on the earth's surface. It could also have given us mastery of ourselves and ensured the success of our individual and social existence. But we have preferred the speculations of eighteenth century philosophic thought to the clear and simple concepts of science. Instead of advancing toward concrete reality, we have stuck fast in abstractions. Undoubtedly, concrete reality is difficult to grasp and our minds are glad to take the line of least resistance. Perhaps it is man's natural sloth which makes him choose the simplicity of the abstract rather than the complexity of the concrete. It is less arduous to hymn the praises of formulas or to drowse over principles than to find out laboriously how things are made and by what means they can be manipulated. It is easier to argue than to observe. As everyone knows, few observations and much discussion are conducive to error: much observation and little discussion to truth. But there are far more minds capable of constructing syllogisms than of accurately grasping the concrete. That is why humanity has always delighted in playing with abstractions even though abstractions give man an incomplete and, at times, totally false vision of reality. Something which is logically true may be empirically false. Are not the cosmologies of Aristotle and St. Thomas entirely erroneous? The geometry of Riemann is no less logical than that of Euclid; the fact remains that it does not apply to our world. If one is not to take false steps in pursuit of the real, it is essential to base oneself, not on the visions of the mind but on the results of observation and experience.

The democratic nations fail to recognize the value of scientific concepts in the organization of communal life. They put their trust in ideologies, those twin daughters of the rationalism of the Age of Enlightenment. Yet neither Liberalism nor Marxism bases itself on an exhaustive observation of reality. The fathers of Liberalism, Voltaire and Adam Smith, had just as arbitrary and incomplete a view of the human world as Ptolemy had of the stellar system. The same applies to those who signed the Declaration of Independence, to the authors of the Declaration of the Rights of Man and of the Citizen as also to Karl Marx and Engels.

The principles of the Communist Manifesto are, in fact, like those of the French Revolution, philosophical views and not scientific concepts. The Liberal bourgeois and the Communist worker share the same belief in the primacy of economics. This belief is inherited from the philosophers of the eighteenth century. It takes no account of the scientific knowledge of the mental and physiological activities of man we possess today nor of the environment which these activities need for their ideal development. Such knowledge shows that primacy belongs not to economics, but to man's own humanity. Instead of trying to find how to organize the State as a function of the human, we are content to declaim the principles of the Declaration of Independence and of the French Revolution. According to these principles, the State is, above all, the guardian of property; the head servant of banking, industry and commerce.

The liberty enjoyed by the majority of men does not belong to the economic, intellectual or moral order. The dispossessed have merely the liberty to go from one slum or one public house to another. They are free to read the lies of one paper rather than another, to listen to opposing forms of radio propaganda and, finally, to vote. Politically they are free; economically they are slaves. Democratic liberty exists only for those who possess something. It allows them to increase their wealth and to enjoy all the various goods of this world. It is only fair to admit that, thanks to it, Capitalism has achieved a vast expansion of wealth and a general improvement in health and in the material conditions of life. But it has, at the same time, created the proletariat. Thus it has deprived men of the land, encouraged their herding together in factories and appalling dwellings, endangered their physical and mental health and divided nations into mutually hostile social classes. The Encylopedists had a profound respect for the owners of property and despised the poor. The French Revolution was directed against both the aristocracy and the proletariat. It was content to substitute the rat for the lion; the bourgeois for the noble. Now Marxism aims at replacing the bourgeois by the worker. The successor of Capitalism is Bureaucracy. Like Liberalism, Marxism arbitrarily gives first place to economics. It allows a theoretical liberty only to the proletariat and suppresses all other classes. The real world is far more complex than the abstraction envisaged by Marx and Engels.

Universal suffrage springs from belief in the equality of individuals. This belief is, however, merely a fantasy of our imagination. One individual is equal to another only in the sense that he is a man and not a gibbon or a chimpanzee. Here again, one may ask whether certain creatures, born of a man and a woman, really possess a human personality. Can an anencephalous monster be said to be a person? Should we consider an idiot, whose mental activity is inferior to that of a dog, a human being? The confusion of symbol and fact has led us to give every individual the same prerogatives. We have not grasped the fact that, though men can be considered equal from the philosophical point of view, they cannot be considered so from the scientific. Many individuals, both in France and America, never get beyond the psychological age of ten and the majority of us never attain full mental maturity. It is, nevertheless, these submen who, thanks to universal suffrage, set the tone in the nation's politics. We have not known how to refute the principles whose application has led to such consequences. The substitution of the contract for the statute, brought about by the French Revolution, is based on a vision of the mind, not on knowledge of reality. Human labor is not something which can be bought like any other commodity. It is an error to depersonalize the thinking and feeling being who operates the machine and to reduce him, in industrial enterprise, to mere "manpower." *Homo Oeconomicus* is a fantasy of our imagination and has no existence in the concrete world.

Our ancestors of the French Revolution sincerely believed in the existence of the rights of man and of the citizen. It never occurred to them that such rights have never

been verified by observation and that they are merely constructions of the mind. The truth is that man has no rights:
what he does have is needs. These needs are observable and
measurable. It is necessary to the success of life that they
should be satisfied. Rights are a philosophical principle;
needs, a scientific concept. In the organization of our collective life, we have preferred our intellectual whims to the
data of science. The triumph of ideologies ratifies the defeat
of civilization.

3 | The Disease of Civilization.—How It Affects the Individual.

The symptoms of this malady are complex. They manifest
themselves simultaneously in the individual, in society and
in the race.

The individual has adapted himself ill to the moral climate in which modern democracy forces him to live. The
mental level has not risen concurrently with the progress of
medicine, hygiene and education. Ever since intemperance,
irresponsibility and the search for comfort have become in
some sort the guiding principles of conduct, nervous resistance, the capacity for effort and even intelligence have diminished. The enormous sums spent by the United States on
public education have not produced the desired result: According to the National Committee of Mental Hygiene, at
least 40,000 children are too stupid to follow the classes. Il-
literates are still very numerous. Herbes' famous investiga-
tion in 1917 on the officers and men of the American Army,
showed that 46 per cent of them were below the mental age
of thirteen.

It is probable that a study of the French population, particularly in certain villages of Normandy and Brittany, would reveal a similar situation. But here we have no statistics which would permit us to compare the chronological and psychological ages of schoolchildren. We must not be deluded about the importance of the examinations with which young people are overloaded. School certificate, matriculation, even university degrees are not a proof of intelligence. Many young people of poor mental caliber manage to pass these examinations. The adult population comprises a great many abnormal persons. In the United States there are possibly thirty million individuals who are unadapted or unadaptable to modern life. In France, numbers of the unemployed are too unintelligent, ignorant or ill to work. A quarter of them show themselves incapable of any activity whatsoever. This means that normal people have to bear the burden of the defectives and the parasites. The majority owes its daily bread to the work of the minority. By an odd aberration, we are more solicitous about our backward children than about our gifted ones.

This general lowering of intelligence and common sense appears to be due to the influence of wine, spirits and excess of all kinds; in fact, to lack of moral discipline. There is a definite relation between the alcoholism of a community and its intellectual decay. (Of all nations addicted to science, France is the one which drinks most wine and least often wins the Nobel Prize.) Certainly the movies, the radio and the absurd complexity of the school curriculum also contribute to the critical state of the French mind. But, undoubtedly, intemperance is one of the main causes of the downward trend of this people once famous as the most intelligent in the world.

There are, at the same time, grave disorders in the non-intellectual activities of the mind; even an atrophy of certain of these activities. Feeling, as much as intellect, has been profoundly affected by the pursuit of profit, sensual satisfaction and amusement. Absence of moral sense, dishonesty, cowardice and intemperance bring about a simultaneous disorder in the affective, intellectual and organic functions. In France, these dislocations of the personality are particularly frequent and pronounced. The Frenchman, though often highly gifted, is apt to display himself as a narrow and petty being. There are, of course, numbers of individuals who are intelligent, healthy and highly moral. There are also large and robust families. In many of the oldest, hereditary potentialities have remained intact. Side by side with idiots, madmen and criminals, one finds admirable artists, great scholars, marvelous inventors and heroes. Christianity is far from being dead. Today, as in the first centuries of its history, the Church continues to produce apostles of charity, mystics and saints. These are undeniable facts and they give us legitimate grounds for hope. But can the high intellectual and moral development of the few make up for the corruption and stupidity of the many? When Greece was conquered by Rome, did she not pride herself on the presence of Polybus and Archimedes? France was once the largest, richest, bravest and most intelligent nation in Europe. The British Empire dominated the world by its gigantic power. The United States lived in a state of hitherto unparalleled prosperity. What factor, other than degeneration, could have been powerful enough to bring such extraordinary disasters on the people of the West?

Optimism is undoubtedly an attractive state of mind. It is tempting to deny the existence of evil since denying it obviates the need to fight it. On the other hand, a clear vision of wrong spurs us to action. We can only get on our feet again if we realize that we have fallen. We have to

admit the fact that we have not known how to guide ourselves.

Do sudden disasters bring back a sense of reality to
those who have lost it? It is essential that the democracies
should understand that they are suffering from the same
sickness as France and that the same fate awaits them.

It is not the first time that this sickness has appeared in
the world. It has already manifested itself at a certain moment in the history of all the great peoples of antiquity. As
Dean Inge once wrote, civilization is a disease which is invariably fatal.

4 | *Consequences of the Revolt on Individual Life.—As-
pects of Liberty.—The Search for Profit.—Satisfaction
of the Appetites and Amusement.—The Reign of
Fantasy.*

Having abandoned our traditional rules we have not known
how to organize our individual life according to new ideas.
We were passionately in love with liberty. The majority of
us took a positive pleasure in the disorder and indifference
which inevitably follow the throwing off of all constraint.
But, beyond the traditional discipline, we have not found
the Promised Land of the fathers of materialistic Liberalism. Very few of us have the time or the taste for medita-
tion. For those who have, however, the freedom engendered
by the progress of rationalism, science and technology does
not show the shining countenance our forefathers attributed
to it in advance. Emancipated man is by no means compara-
ble to an eagle soaring in the immensity of the sky. He far
more closely resembles a dog escaped from its kennel and
dashing hither and thither among the traffic. He can indeed,

like the dog, do exactly as he pleases and go wherever he wants. He is none the less lost because he does not know where to go or how to protect himself from the dangers which surround him. How is he to discover once again the moral security his ancestors knew when they built the Gothic cathedrals on the soil of Europe? Those men were part of a society in which each had his place and from which none was excluded; where the humblest as well as the greatest knew how he should behave, whither he was bound and what was the true meaning of life and death. Nowadays we have left forever the little house which made up the universe of our forefathers. We have left the trees and the plants, our brothers the animals, and the sweet valley where, in the misty dawn, the angels of the Lord sometimes walked at our side. We are content to be imperceptible microbes, vegetating on a grain of dust which itself is lost in the empty heavens. We are strangers in this mysterious universe where our joys, our desires, our anguish wake no single echo; where, in no realm, do we ever encounter the spirit.

Nevertheless, it is impossible for us to ignore the existence of the world of lovers, saints and poets. But this spiritual world differs profoundly from the physical from which, none the less, it is inseparable. In the shoreless ocean of reality, man finds only what he seeks. St. Francis of Assisi found God; Einstein, the laws of the cosmos. God can only be encountered outside the dimensions of space and time; beyond the intellect, in that indefinable realm, which according to Ruysbroek the Admirable, can only be penetrated by love and longing. For the majority of men, the universe of the physicists and that of the mystics are alike sealed. The first is symbolized by mathematical formulas which we do not yet understand and the second is described in terms of medieval philosophy which have lost their meaning for us.

Both these languages are only intelligible to a few initiates. Today there is no communication between the realm of the soul and the realm of matter. No one has attempted to do for us what St. Thomas Aquinas successfully did for the men of the Middle Ages. Yet we need a coherent universe in which each person can once again find his place; where the spiritual and material are not in separate compartments; and where we know how to find our way. We are beginning to realize that it is dangerous to travel the roads of life without compass or guide.

It is strange that the realization of this danger should not have induced us to find a means of organizing our life in a rational way. True, the number of those who clearly perceive the acuteness of the danger is, even now, infinitesimal. Hardly anyone understands that the policy of laissez-faire produces as disastrous results in the life of individuals as in that of nations. The Church alone continues to fight for the maintaining of strict moral rules but this fight is far from being victorious. The vast majority nowadays is determined to live as it pleases. Intoxicated by the material facilities which the immense progress of technology is able to offer it, it has no intention of foregoing a single privilege of modern civilization. Like the water of a stream which loses itself indifferently in lake, desert or marsh, life follows the slope of our desires and flows into every form of mediocrity or corruption. Today its current is set toward profit, amusement and sensual satisfaction.

In the mental climate created by Liberalism, the idea of profit has invaded our whole field of consciousness. Wealth appears as the supreme good; success is measured in units of money. Business affairs are sacred. The search for material gain has spread from banking, industry and commerce to all other human activities. The mainspring of our actions is the desire to gain some personal and, above all, pecuniary advantage. Equally, we want to satisfy our vanity by promotions, titles, decorations and social position. This self-interest is dissimulated with subtle hypocrisy; it appears as altruism or disguises itself in various ingenious ways. In the army and the university, in administration and law, we witness long-term plots against the dangerous rival; carefully camouflaged betrayals, stabs in the back in the dark. Honor has become an anachronism. Those who devote themselves to an ideal and who work without self-interest are considered hypocrites or fools. The love of gain penetrates everywhere. It operates in that charitable lady whose secret aim is not to help the poor but to be president of a committee, to be decorated with the Legion of Honor or, more prosaically, to make a profit out of opening a canteen. It operates in that great doctor who is always insisting to his pupils and patients the efficacy of some remedy when, all the while, he is being secretly paid by its manufacturers. What of that learned professor whose effort is directed, not to the advance of knowledge, but to a chair in the Academy and the discreet financial perquisites of authority? What of those doctors who, in their public pronouncements and even in their private practice, display an astonishing moral decadence? What of that undergraduate who bribes someone in the know to tell him beforehand the subject of an examination essay? Or of that schoolboy selling vitamin sweets, given to him by his school, on the black market? Too often the vulgar and cruel face of self-interest hides behind the mask of devotion, knowledge, charity and even innocence. We have this passion for gain because money can procure anything. First and foremost, it purveys power. Nearly every man can be bought: if not with money itself, at least with those things which only those who have it can give.

Money can satisfy all our desires because the desires themselves are base.

Our idea of living is the blind satisfaction of appetite. We eat to excess, without regard to the laws of nutrition. Our food is ill-chosen and often ill-prepared. Women have forgotten how to cook. Civilized people have formed the habit of daily intoxicating themselves with overlarge doses of tea, coffee, spirits, wine, cider and tobacco. Thanks to commercial advertising, the people of the West have created new needs for themselves. The craving for alcohol is partly responsible for our modern decadence. Civilized people are also at the mercy of their sexual appetites; appetites whose perversion is so harmful to old and young. But there are other, subtler appetites, less apparently harmful than sexual excesses or the craving for drink. Such are the love of denigration and lying; delight in duplicity, a taste for sophistry, verbosity, verbalism and witty backbiting. This spiritual immoderation is almost as dangerous as the ridiculous pleasure of excessive drinking.

Western civilization is distinguished by its worship of the intellect. Yet there is no reason to give intellect pride of place over feeling. It is obviously wrong to classify young people by examinations in which moral and organic values have no place. To make thought itself the goal of thought is a kind of mental perversion. Intellectual and sexual activity alike should be exercised in a natural way. The function of the intellect is not to satisfy itself but to contribute, along with the other organic and mental functions, to the satisfaction of the individual's total needs.

Life that has neither aim nor discipline naturally tends to wander off into the morass of amusement. The brute satisfaction of appetite can have a certain grandeur. But nothing is more absurd than an existence spent in amusing oneself. What is the point of living if living consists in dancing, driving frenziedly about in cars, going to the movies and listening to the radio? Such amusements uselessly dissipate the leisure which the workers have slowly and painfully acquired, thanks to machinery and modern methods of production. That vast labor has procured them four extra hours to their day; precious hours which, well used, would allow them to educate themselves; to develop themselves physically, mentally and spiritually. Instead, amusement absorbs every free moment left over by office or factory. Many young workers spend three or four evenings a week at the movies, the dance hall or the music hall. Idle chatter or silly novels take up the rest of their spare time. Another method of frittering away one's life is listening to the lies and absurdities of the radio. Some schoolchildren, it seems, can only learn their lessons while listening to the radio. The radio, like the movies, imposes complete passivity on its addicts. Amusement is in opposition to life, for life is action.

To sum up, during the period between the two world wars, all the ancient rules of conduct were thrown overboard. Everywhere, fantasy ruled. Our collective life was inspired by Liberal ideology, that fantasy of the mind. In our individual life we pursued the fantasies of our senses and our intellect. Nevertheless we knew that the laws of nature existed. We should have deduced that human nature too was subject to certain rules. We thought ourselves independent of universal order and free to act as we pleased. Eating, sleeping, copulation, the possession of a car or a radio set, dancing, going to the movies and making money seemed to us the whole destiny of man. In a cloud of cigarette smoke, in the lazy bliss engendered by alcohol, everyone, in his own way, enjoyed life.

CHAPTER TWO

The Necessity of Obeying Natural Laws

1 | *Order of the World.—Natural Laws and Those Invented by Man.—Character of Natural Laws.—Prediction of Phenomena and Mastery of Nature.*

An evident order can be observed in the world. The sun never fails to rise. Night invariably succeeds day, and spring winter. Living beings, like inanimate ones, are constructed in a certain way and are definitely related to each other. Life conforms to its cosmic background and the cosmic background to life. All things found on earth and in the heavens are made up of the combination of less than one hundred elements. Though infinitely numerous, they are all related and each behaves in the mode ordained by its structure, for nature is incapable of caprice.

From time immemorial, men have been dimly aware of these facts. Long before the dawn of stoic thought, Heraclitus had already grasped the idea of an order in the universe and the need to adapt ourselves to this order. Science was born of the belief that reality was essentially uniform. All research begins with an act of faith in the rational ordering of nature. The great success of science has proved that, far from being a superstition, such a belief was a profound and precise intuition of the structure of the cosmos. It is because there is nothing fantastic about the cosmos that science has been able to develop. Little by little, it has revealed the modes of behavior of the inanimate world and, to a certain extent, those of living beings. With Aristotle, it first described and classified phenomena. From qualitative, science then became quantitative. With Galileo, Newton and Lavoisier it came to its full stature.

Little by little, it perceived the hidden uniformity beneath the complex variety of the surface. It discovered the existence of constant relationships between varying phenomena. These relationships are natural laws: laws of matter, life and thought. The two last are far from being as simple as those which govern inert matter. They cannot yet be expressed in mathematical terms. Yet the leucocyte stretching out its pseudopods toward the bacterium, the wailing newborn baby and the scientist experimenting in his laboratory are no more due to a caprice of nature than tide, wind or avalanche. Investigated with scientific method, they all testify to the underlying order of things.

Natural laws differ profoundly from man-made ones. They are discovered, not invented. Like the spring at the bottom of the well, they exist before they are discovered. Our civil and military codes are mere collections of regulations. Natural laws express the very structure of things and constitute their functional aspect. Thus the function of the eye is to project the image of exterior objects on the extension of the brain which is inserted into it. Structure and function are two aspects of one and the same object. Natural laws are immanent in both animate and inanimate beings. If the substratum of the universe is a creative intelligence, they reveal an aspect of this intelligence. Marcus Aurelius thought the world was like the body of God. Too many human laws are, on the contrary, merely external. They represent only social conventions, frail and arbitrary products of our own reason. What is lawful in one country is not necessarily so in another. "Keep to the right," says the French highway code; "Keep to the left," says the English. In the sight of such laws, all men are by no means equal. The rich and powerful can infringe them with impunity. The natural laws, on the contrary, are universal and inexorable. In no country can they be disobeyed without penalty. Nor do they ever warn the transgressor; the punishment is as silent as the command.

On certain days of the year, the Athenian Assembly had the task of revising its laws. Social conventions are always transitory. But natural laws have existed since the origin of the universe and will last to its end. The speed of light will never change. Before the laws of gravity, all men are equal. We shall never be able, of our own accord, to walk on water or fly in air. As long as the moon circles the earth, there will be tides. Nothing will stop a chemical reaction from doubling its velocity each time the temperatures rises 10 degrees centigrade. Today, as one hundred thousand years ago, glycogene turns into lactic acid in a working muscle. When the muscle becomes acid, fatigue will supervene. A calorie will always equal 425 kilogrammeters. In the same way, the laws of heredity are invariable. Madmen and mental defectives will continue to be engendered by madmen and mental defectives. The tissues of human beings are of such a kind that they will always deteriorate under the influence of alcohol. Natural laws, then, do not, like civil law, constitute a contingent aspect of reality; they are a necessary aspect of everything which exists around us and in ourselves.

With a knowledge of these laws, we can predict phenomena or provoke their appearance at will. Such knowledge has made men masters of the earth. But order does not manifest itself so clearly in the whole of nature. Our mind cannot penetrate every realm of reality with equal ease. It excels in discovering the secrets of inert matter and in constructing mathematical abstractions. But, since it loves simplicity and life is infinitely complex, it finds it far harder to understand living phenomena. Mechanics, physics and chemistry are far more advanced than physiology, psychology or the social sciences. We understand atoms and stars better than our own minds.

There is a hierarchy in natural laws. At the top come those which express complete uniformity in the behavior of things. Such, for example, are the laws of gravity and of the conservation of matter and the two laws of the conservation and dissipation of energy. Lower down we find the biological laws such as those of adaptation and heredity. These are far from having reached that degree of abstraction, precision and beauty which enable the physical laws to be defined in algebraical formulas. They can only be considered as expressing the tendencies of certain bodily activities.

Even more imperfect are the laws of psychology. Yet the modalities of reason or feeling play as essential a part in the world as the law of gravity for they characterize the greatest and most mysterious energy on earth. On the lowest step of the hierarchy stand the laws of sociology. Many of these are mere hypotheses, for sociology is still a conjectural science. Thus we are far from knowing all the parts of reality with equal certitude.

Phenomena can only be predicted with certainty in the realm of physics or chemistry. We can foretell, without possibility of error, the exact moment of the next eclipse of the sun and what will happen if we mix sulphuric acid with carbonate of calcium. But we cannot determine in advance the time when a given individual will die or what effect victory or defeat will have on the future of a nation.

Perhaps human intelligence has not yet reached the period of evolution when it will become capable of grasping the real under its multiple forms. Perhaps we need only employ better and more patient methods for natural laws to reveal themselves with equal clarity in all domains. But our ignorance should not lead us to believe that order extends only to one part of the world.

Undoubtedly, the success of moral and social life depends on laws as definite, though more complex, as those which relate to the partial pressures of gases in mixtures or to the propagation of light rays. But we do not yet know those laws.

We must not forget that our ancestors divined an order in the universe, but that they never discovered its laws. The moderns have discovered the laws of physics, chemistry and physiology. Yet perhaps we shall remain forever incapable of formulating those laws of human relations whose existence we suspect today. In its slow ascent toward the light, the spirit only gradually acquires the strength to grasp the obscure mechanisms of the harmony of the world.

2 | *Man's Place on the Earth.—Conformity of the Cosmic Environment to Life and of Life to the Cosmic Environment.—Reciprocal Dependence of Bodily and Mental Activities.—Man Forms Part of Nature.*

In conducting our life, we must never let ourselves ignore the natural order of things. True, we still preserve the illusion of being privileged among living beings and of escaping the common law. The sense of being free gives us a deceptive confidence. We believe that our situation is vastly superior to that of plants, trees and animals. It is important for us to have a clear idea of our true place in nature.

The human body, as we have known since Aristotle, is an autonomous unit in which all the parts have mutual functional relations and exist to serve the whole. It is made up of tissues, blood and consciousness. These three elements are distinct, but inseparable from each other. They are equally inseparable, though distinct, from the physical, chemical and psychological milieu in which we are immersed. All the substances which make up blood and tissues come directly or indirectly from this environment through the medium of plants and animals. The greater part of our body is composed of the water of rain, springs and rivers. This interior water holds in solution definite proportions of minerals which originate in the earth. It constitutes the substratum of the cells and the blood. Like earth and sea water, it contains sodium, potassium, magnesium, calcium, iron, copper and a quantity of rarer elements such as manganese, zinc and arsenic which come to us from animal flesh, milk, cereals, vegetables, tubers and roots. Plants and animals also supply the nitrogenous matter; the fats, sugars, salts and vitamins we need to build up, maintain and restore our tissues. The chemical components of our bodies are identical with those which make up the sun, moon and stars. There is no difference between the oxygen in the atmosphere of Mars and the oxygen we breathe. The hydrogen contained in the molecule of the glycogene of liver and our muscles and the calcium of our bones are the same as the hydrogen and the calcium of the flames in the atmosphere of the sun filmed by Mac Math. The iron in the red globules of our blood is the same as that of the meteorites. The atoms of sodium which float like fine mist in interstellar space could be used just as well by our tissues as the salt in our food. In fact, all the chemical elements of which our bodies are made up come from the cosmos; from earth, air and water. Those elements behave in the same way whether inside the body or out. Claude Bernard taught us that the laws of physiology are fundamentally the same as those of mechanics, physics and chemistry. Things do not vary in their mode of being: the laws of capillary attraction, osmosis and hydrodynamics remain true in the heart of our tissues. It is possible however, on Donnan's hypothesis, that certain statistical laws cease to operate in certain cells so small that they contain only a few protein macro molecules.

Thus our body is a fragment of the cosmos, arranged in a very special way, but obeying the same laws as the rest of the world. It is made up of the same elements as its physical ambience. Moreover man is functionally related to his environment. Each is adjusted to the other in such a way that one could say the environment is the lock and man the key. The surface of the earth presents a set of physical and chemical conditions which are exceptional in the universe and eminently suited to our existence. Our planet retains about it an atmosphere dense enough for living creatures to breathe the oxygen they need even on high mountains. This same atmosphere protects plants and animals from cold and from the harmful rays of the sun. And the attraction the earth exercises on all bodies makes us adhere to its soil in the degree necessary to our mode of life.

On the surface of Jupiter we should be immobilized by our weight. On the moon we should be too light. As Henderson has shown, the cosmic milieu is adapted to life mainly on account of the peculiar properties of three elements: oxygen, hydrogen and carbon, which compose water and carbonic acid. Water and carbonic acid stabilize the temperature of the earth. Moreover water liquefies nearly all chemical elements. Once liquefied, these elements penetrate everywhere and serve as food for plants. Hydrogen, oxygen and carbonic acid are the most active of all elements. They create the greatest number of compounds and the most complex molecular structures. Thanks to water which brings them the majority of chemical elements in solution, plants and animals can prepare the complicated nutriment man needs. This environment conforms to life and vice versa. Life uses two processes in this conforming. The first consists in absorbing or assimilating the environment. Thus the organism absorbs oxygen from the air and assimilates nourishing substances. The second consists in reacting against the environment and in adjusting itself to it. The adjustment comes about through an effort of the great adaptive systems.[1] The repetition of this effort increases the power of these systems; i.e. the vessels, nerve centers, muscles, glands, heart and all the organs. This is why the individual needs to be in constant struggle with his environment if he is to develop to his highest capacity. Hard conditions of life are indispensable to bringing out the best in human personality.

Learned men often made the strange mistake of observing natural phenomena as if they themselves stood outside nature. The fact is that they are part of a material system composed of observer and observed.

True, our mind is not confined in the four dimensions of space and time.[2] Though we are immersed in the cosmos, we feel we have the power to liberate ourselves from it. In some way we do not yet understand, the mind can escape from the physical *continuum*. Nevertheless, it remains inseparable from the body and thus from the physical world to which it is subject. The blood plasma has only to be deprived of certain chemical substances for the noblest aspira-

[1] *Man the Unknown.*
[2] *Ibid.*

tions of the soul to vanish. When, for example, the thyroid gland stops secreting thyroxin into the blood vessels, intelligence, sense of good and evil, sense of beauty and religious feeling disappear. Increase or diminution of calcium both upset mental balance. Chronic alcoholism disintegrates the personality. If, as Madame Collum did, one completely cuts out manganese from the diet of a female rat, the rat loses its maternal instinct. On the other hand, if one administers prolactine (a particular extract of the pituitary gland) to virgin rats, the animals adopt young rats, build nests for them and cherish them with the utmost care. If no young rats are available, they will devote their mother-love to newly-hatched pigeons. Our feelings are definitely and deeply influenced by certain illnesses. A mild dose of sleeping sickness may result in a total change of personality. When the *spirochæta pallida,* the parasite of syphilis, begins to invade the brain, it sometimes illuminates the intelligence with flashes of genius. The state of the mind is conditioned by that of the body.

On the surface of the earth we are beings analogous to other beings; nearer, however, to plants and animals than to rocks and rivers. We are closely related to the higher mammals, particularly gibbons and chimpanzees, but our minds are vastly superior to theirs. Thanks to our intelligence, we are free to act as we choose. It is this sense of freedom which gives us the illusion of being independent of nature. Though it is true that we are free, we are, all the same, subject to the natural order of things. If we wish, we can ignore nature's laws. We can get out of a boat in order to walk on the water, we can jump from the top of the Empire State Building, we can take hashish and live in a marvelous dream world or give ourselves up to the corruption of modern civilization. But we can never break the bonds which bind us to the earth from which we spring. The will of man will always be impotent to alter the structure of the universe. Since we are part of nature, we must conform to her laws, as Epictetus taught. We must be that which it is in our very essence to be.

3 | *How Living Beings Fit into Nature.—The Role of Instinct.—Coming of Liberty.—Role of Intelligence and Will.*

How do autonomous animals fit into the order of the world? All things behave according to their structure. Since there are vast numbers of things, their interconnections are infinitely complex. Animals, though ignorant of themselves and their environment, find their way with marvelous precision through the labyrinth of reality. They seem to possess, as Fabre believed, an innate sense of the harmony of the universe. The same cannot be said of man. Life seems to have chosen two different methods of entering the world and developing itself. One method is instinct; the other intelligence and will.

All living beings, except man, possess a kind of innate knowledge of the world and of themselves. This instinct forces them to fit themselves completely and securely into the natural order. They are not free to make mistakes. Only beings endowed with reason are fallible and, consequently, perfectible. Insect communities prospered as well ten thousand years ago as they do today. In the higher animals such as anthropoid apes, elephants and dogs, instinct is surrounded by a fringe of intelligence. But, in the fundamental acts of life, intelligence is always eclipsed by instinct. Unlike a woman, a bitch never makes a mistake in caring for her puppies. Birds know when to build their nests; bees know the proper diet on which to rear queens, workers and drones. Since instinct is automatic, animals are not free to live according to their own whims as men are. They adapt themselves as blindly and as precisely to their environment as the cells of our organs do to the physicochemical conditions of the blood and the tissue fluids. The animal and its environment could almost be compared to a perfectly balanced physical system. When our ancestors were still wild animals, instinct was their supreme guide.

By slow degrees, the advent of consciousness brought about the dissolution of instinct. Undoubtedly a fringe of instinct still surrounds the human intelligence. But it is not powerful enough to give us a firm grasp of the external world and to suit our behavior to its conditions. Man cannot, like the wolf, find his way in a dark forest without a guide. Neither can he distinguish friend from foe or the living from the dead at first sight. He is liberated from the automatism of tropisms and reflexes. He is free; he has acquired the privilege of being able to make mistakes. It is for him to choose his own way among all those offered, and to make himself follow the one he has chosen. All he can now rely on to direct his life is the conscious effort of his mind. And mind, as a guide, is less sure than instinct. Man still does not know how to behave. He has never succeeded in building an enduring civilization. One might say that consciousness has not yet evolved to the point where it is capable of ordering our collective life as efficiently as instinct governs the collective life of ants. No task, therefore, is more important than to increase the strength of the mind. Mind (or spirit, if we prefer the term) is at once intellect and feeling, reason and heart, logical and nonlogical activity. To adapt ourselves to reality we need feeling quite as much as intelligence. Intelligence grasps the external world and the interrelation of things, but does not drive us to action.

Intellectual activity consists of observing, remembering, comparing, judging and experimenting. First it makes an inventory of things; then it analyzes the influences these things exercise on each other. Thus it studies the influence of diet on health, of warm weather on the putrefaction of food, of bad temper on domestic harmony and numberless other relations of cause and effect. Knowledge thus obtained is the only reliable kind we have. We have to initiate ourselves into the essential nature of our body, our mind and our environment; to make contact with concrete reality. We have to learn what to eat, how to work and how to rest. We have to learn how to behave toward our families, friends and fellow workers; how to cooperate with our neighbor. Only from the data of observation and experience can we derive any notion of how to fit ourselves into the scheme of things. Thus it is the duty of each one of us to acquire this necessary knowledge of ourselves and our environment.

4 | *Reality at Our Level.—Difficulty of Grasping Reality.* *—Taste for Ideologies.—Aspects of Reality.*

Reality is the most difficult thing for the human mind to grasp. This vital knowledge comes only from observation and experiment and the effort these require is repugnant to us. It is easier to read the papers, listen to the radio and go to the movies. Most people are incapable of close contact with themselves, with each other or, indeed, with anything at all. They are the victims of their education and their habits. Their only intellectual formation has been acquired by cramming for examinations. In the artificial life of the factory and the office, they have never looked reality in the face. They ignore the beauty of the virgin snow, the noon-

day hush on the still cornfields, the anguish of the sick in
lonely farmhouses. They are incapable of observing exactly
what happens in and about them. Yet the reality we need so
desperately to know is not made up of notions picked up
from books and newspapers but the immediate data of observation and experience. These data can only be used in
the form of abstractions which remain very close to the concrete: as simple concepts belonging to the class of operational concepts we have mentioned before. Such concepts
are as necessary to the conduct of life as to the progress of
science. They are the only instruments which permit the
mind to find its way in the real world with the certainty of
instinct.

Reality has several aspects. They are created either by the
technique employed in the analysis of phenomena or by the
scale on which these observations are made. The techniques
which reveal our spiritual activities, though far less precise,
are just as important as those designed to analyze organic
ones. Everything we know about the universe and about
ourselves derives from two distinct sciences: that of the in-
organic world where physics and chemistry overlap and that
of life which includes psychology and sociology as well as
anatomy, physiology and genetics. Whether we discover in
man a material structure, physiological activities or intellectual and moral ones, depends on whether we are using the
technique of anatomy, physiology or psychology. The most
direct of all analytical techniques is introspection. The examination of the self by the self brings us face to face with
something different from anything which has existed since
the beginning of the universe; with an event which has
never happened before and can never happen again. We
come up against that thing at once fixed and changing, mysterious and familiar, material and spiritual, which is ourself. The vision of this unique being, arrived at by introspec-

tion, constitutes for us the most certain and least variable aspect of reality. Such observations are always made from the same point of view since the observer is himself the object observed. They are made direct, with no apparatus to increase or diminish the clearness of vision. Although no microscope or telescope exists to explore our own consciousness, the habit of self-examination sharpens our insight. We gain a progressively profounder knowledge of the characteristics and particular trends of our own personality. All other aspects of reality, whether of our own bodies or of anything else in the physical world, can only be observed at second hand and at different and variable levels. The aspect of the same object varies according to the standpoint of the observer. The Statue of Liberty illuminating the world in New York harbor loses all significance if one sees it from too near or too far. Seen from its foot, it appears an almost shapeless mass of bronze. If one flies several hundred feet above it, both statue and island become a mere meaningless dot on the water. The skin of the face, seen by the painter, differs profoundly from what the anatomist sees when he examines it through a microscope. An observation made from a given point of view is neither more nor less true than that made from another. The idea of the blood which we derive from physicochemistry is not better than the one we derive from histology. One expresses the molecular aspect of the blood and the other the cellular. From the human point of view, blood is simply the red liquid which runs out when we cut ourselves. The ideas derived from observations on one plane are not always applicable on another. The principles of Euclid are true as regards the surface of the earth but not in the totality of the universe which appears to be non-Euclidean. The laws of pure mechanics do not apply to the interatomic world. A concept is only valid on the level from which it was derived.

Of what kind of reality, then, do we so urgently need knowledge to conduct our lives? Of reality on our own level, such as it presents itself to our ordinary experience. For us, the real aspect of a poplar tree is what we perceive when we walk in its shade, not what we see from an airplane high above its summit. Our cosmic universe is far closer to that of our ancestors who lived when the Gothic cathedrals were still white than to that of Planck, Einstein or Broglie. For us it is still true that the sun goes round the earth and that the earth is the center of the universe. What is real from our point of view are the joys and sorrows of daily life and human beings in all the circumstances of their passage through this world. Lovers walking in the moonlight, the mother smiling at her child, the peasant harnessing his oxen, the clerk scraping a living at his desk, the baby we once were and the corpse we shall one day be . . . these are real for us. Yet reality from our point of view stretches beyond the physical *continuum*, beyond the four dimensions of space and time into that immaterial world poets and saints have revealed to us. A hero's sacrifice has a beauty as vivid as that of sunrise on snowy mountains. Grace illuminates the face of one chosen by God with an interior light as real as that of dawn. Since, in fact, the world of matter is inseparable from that of spirit, we must learn to understand both. The laws we need above all to know are not those of the stellar or the interatomic universe but the fundamental tendencies of things as they are revealed to us on our own level by observation and experience. These constitute the aspect of reality which is essential for us to bear in mind in every circumstance of our lives.

	Divorce of Man from Reality.—How Modern Civili-
5	*zation Has Disobeyed Natural Laws.—Response of*
	Life.—Explanation of Our Troubles.

Man has only grasped one aspect of reality. He has plucked the forbidden fruit from the tree of knowledge before it was ripe. It gave us the knowledge of all things save ourselves.

Now we are advancing on the road of time, dependent on the progress of technology and completely unconcerned about the elementary needs of our bodies and minds. Though we are still immersed in matter, we fancy ourselves independent of it. We wish to ignore the fact that our survival depends on behaving in the way demanded by our own structure and that of the things about us. For centuries, civilized humanity has been plunging deeper and deeper into this error.

The exclusively intellectual formation of the young violates an essential law of the development of the mind. The human spirit displays nonrational as well as rational activities. Activities not specifically rational, such as the moral, esthetic and mystical senses, play a most important part in the development of personality. We have made the mistake of neglecting the affective formation of the child.

We still do not grasp that physiological development is inseparable from the development of the feelings. To accord fully with nature's intentions, education should also concern itself with organic activities and with those mental activities which are not concerned simply with the process of reasoning. Parents and teachers commit still graver sins against life. One essential law for the development of living beings is that of effort. Muscles, vital organs, intelligence and will

can only be strengthened by work. No error can be more
fatal than that of suppressing the voluntary effort of mind
and muscle and the involuntary one of the adaptive systems.
Our ancestral laws of conduct were the expression of a profound intuition of human nature. Christian morality also
imposes rules which are none other than those intended by
life itself. Life has replied to our disobedience to its laws by
estranging itself from us; a reply at once silent and brutal.
Only the most clear-sighted have been aware of the danger.
Slowly, over a long period, life has been working out its
answer.

Less than a century ago, French institutions were the
envy of Europe. France produced the cream of artists, writers and scientists; her riches were constantly increasing: she
was a great nation. Yet already she was showing irrefutable
proofs of decay. By 1830, the malady of civilization was far
advanced among the French, though the definite breakdown
did not come till later. This flight from life was made spontaneously. The human body possesses an almost miraculous
power of standing up to the most adverse circumstances.
When it reaches the limit of its power of adaptation, various
disorders appear: moral corruption, feeble-mindedness, neu-
rosis, criminality and sterility. Like a machine not driven as
its structure demands, it breaks down. You cannot go
straight from top gear into reverse, nor can you run your
engine on sand or water. In conducting one's life, as in driving a car, every mistake brings retribution. Those who transgress natural laws are annihilated by the mere play of the
inherent mechanism of things.

Both the disease of civilization and that of universal war
are inevitable consequences of transgressing natural laws.
The absence of all internal discipline leads to giving up
voluntary effort. It also leads to the abuse of comfort and
to a general softening up of life; hence to the slackening of

our adaptive functions and the suppression of the constant effort imposed on our organs and nerve centers by the un-remitting fight against bad weather, hunger, sleep and fatigue. Yet this effort is the essential condition of the development of our tissues and our minds. Children and young people not brought up to realize the need for effort have become submen too weak to maintain the civilization of their forebears. In such individuals, the intelligence, however cultured, remains frail, superficial and incapable of great creative work. Intelligence, to be strong and well-balanced, needs a sound organic substratum. Moral emancipation and economic changes have confused the specific functions of man and woman. Woman cannot, or will not, carry out her true feminine function; hence the decay in quality as well as quantity in a nation. Our forefathers in the sixteenth century never suspected what the consequences would be for humanity when they so lightly substituted the love of profit for the love of God. Putting economics first brought about the industrial revolution, the rise of Liberalism, a vast increase in wealth and a general improvement in living conditions. These resulted in a huge increase in the population of Europe and a frantic search for primary raw materials and markets. Hence came total war and, finally, chaos. Such was life's reply to man's disobedience.

6 | *Conflict between Natural Laws and Human Liberty. —Necessity for a Voluntary Restriction of Liberty.— The Law of Sacrifice.*

There is no limit to our liberty of thought. Our imagination, too, is as free of all constraint as the wind blowing over the desert sand. Our intelligence can follow logical principles or ignore them, just as it pleases. Everyone has the privilege of being illogical when he wants to. He is also privileged to erect logical constructions which are based on concrete reality, such as Euclidean geometry, or others which have no connection with it, such as the geometry of Riemann. Equally, there is no barrier to the expression of our feelings. We are free to give ourselves up to jealousy, rapacity, pride, intemperance, lust and selfishness; to follow all our impulses and indulge all our appetites. We are almost as free in our actions as in our thoughts and feelings. Man is allowed to behave as he wishes; the vast vista of the possible lies open before him.

Our liberty of thought and action is bounded only by the consequences of those thoughts and deeds. The field of the possible is divided into two sectors by an invisible and immutable frontier. In one sector, our freedom can be safely exercised; in the other it sooner or later brings catastrophe. The frontier is fixed forever by the nature of things; by the structure of ourselves and of the cosmos. Our ancestors possessed a traditional wisdom, a kind of intuition of the dangerous regions, which we now despise. Because we ignore the barrier between the permissible and the forbidden, we cannot use our freedom with impunity.

The aim of the science of living is precisely to demarcate this frontier for us, to show us how to keep on the safe side of it, to teach us, in fact, how to use our freedom in a rational way. It is easy to know what margin of safety is left us by the laws of chemistry and physics. A child soon learns that it cannot walk on a pond like a water beetle or support itself in the air like a butterfly. It learns in good time that fire burns. But it will never realize of its own accord that to eat nothing but meat and cakes is just as dangerous. Many physiological laws are not merely quite unknown to the general public but very imperfectly known to scientists. Most people have only a rudimentary knowledge of themselves. Their notions of hygiene, for example, are extremely sketchy. Napoleon was a victim of this ignorance. If Gambetta was an old man at forty-two, this was undoubtedly due to his having deliberately underfed himself in his youth. The moderns do not realize that education and sociology also have laws, less clearly defined but as sacrosanct as those of physics. They still allow themselves to be guided by philosophers and reformers. They bow to Jean-Jacques Rousseau or John Dewey in the case of education; to Adam Smith, Jeremy Bentham or Karl Marx in the case of sociology.

As the laws of life usually only punish their transgressors after many generations, we have not learned to submit to them as we submit to physical laws like the law of gravity. Modern man is the victim of the tragic conflict between natural law and human liberty. Liberty, like dynamite, is an efficacious but dangerous tool. We have to learn to handle it, and to handle it properly demands intelligence and will. The frontier between the permissible and the forbidden is, as we know, invisible. Instead of wandering at will over the vast plain, we must keep to the track. And this track is narrow, rough and ill-defined. We must, then, voluntarily restrict our freedom if we are to succeed in life.

This opposition between freedom and the natural laws makes asceticism imperative. To avoid disaster to ourselves and our descendants, we must resist many of our impulses, tastes and desires. Sacrifice is a law of life. For a woman, to have children entails an interminable series of sacrifices. To become an athlete, an artist or a scientist involves hard training. Health, strength and longevity can only be attained through the refusal to gratify appetites. Our era began under the very sign of sacrifice, yet sacrifice is not a virtue reserved for saints and heroes. It is a specific need of human life. This need became apparent when liberty took the place of the automatism of instinct for our forebears. Every time man has used the whole of his liberty, he has infringed the natural laws and been severely punished.

Neither philosophers nor theologians should attempt to construct man according to their particular doctrines, whatever those doctrines may be, for man's horizon is always too narrow. It is sheer pride to believe oneself capable of correcting nature, for nature is the work of God. Man should be what his inherited potentialities permit him to be. He must develop the tendencies we humbly attempt to decipher in his body and soul. We have the power to mold youth almost exactly to our own desired pattern, for living matter is infinitely plastic. With good techniques we could construct the man we wished but this product of our doctrines would not be viable. Like ourselves, the creature would sooner or later be engulfed in folly, corruption and chaos. To command nature, we must obey her. The price of success in our personal, social and racial life is humble submission to the immutable nature of things.

CHAPTER THREE

The Fundamental Laws of Human Life

	Laws of Human Life.—These Laws Should Not Be
1	Deduced from Philosophical Principles, but Inferred
	from the Observation of Life Itself.

It is useless to attempt, as we have done hitherto, to deduce these natural laws from philosophical principles or political and social ideologies. Such constructions, however ingenious, must always remain piecemeal views of human activity, pale phantoms of reality. Philosophy is always trying to make a harmonious synthesis of knowledge, to speculate on the origin and nature of things, and to formulate doctrines which will satisfy the aspirations of the soul. But such doctrines are like those luminous shapes which hover above a misty plain; no one can tell whether they are the eternal hills or merely clouds which the wind will soon disperse. No system of thought has yet gained universal adherence. Principles considered eternal by some are not admitted as such by others. Laws of life deduced from such principles are mere suppositions which can never have universal authority. The quarrel between materialists and idealists has been going on for twenty-five centuries and is far from being settled today. Is man matter or spirit or both at once? Are

we to deduce the laws of life from the principles of Zeno
or of Epicurus, from the ideas of St. Thomas Aquinas or
from those of Jeremy Bentham? Is primitive life necessarily
good and modern social life necessarily bad? "Everything is
good as it comes from the hands of the author of life; everything degenerates in the hands of man," wrote Rousseau. In
spite of the success of this doctrine, the noble savage remains a myth.

To the Utilitarians, the principle of the natural identity
of interests appeared to be the fundamental law of economic relations. Today we know that these philosophers
were wrong. Many men believe that the aim of life is the
piling up of wealth; a few that it consists in laying up treas-
ure in heaven "where neither rust nor moth doth corrupt."
To put economics first, as Adam Smith and Karl Marx
taught, involves rules of behavior opposed to those which
derive from giving first place to the spiritual. Principles and
controversies rage furiously about us. No system is sufficiently sure to serve as an indisputable base for our behavior.
The laws of life can no more be deduced from eternal principles than can those of physics. We must renounce the hope
that the logicians, however dexterous, can reveal the rules
of human conduct.

If we are not to deceive ourselves, we must deduce the
laws of life from the observation of life itself, just as we have
deduced the laws of physics and chemistry from observing
inanimate matter. The time has come to corroborate philosophical principles by scientific concepts. Concepts derived
from observation and experiment are solid and can be tested.
In case of doubt, the observations and experiments which
produced the concept can be repeated. Only an idiot would
deny, for example, the existence of the laws of heredity and
adaptation. Unfortunately, the study of man demands the
knowledge of several exact techniques. To grasp human

activities in all their complexity we need the methods of anatomy, physiology, physics, chemistry, pathology, medicine, pedagogy, psychology, economics and sociology. Before any phenomenon can be considered the expression of a fundamental mode of life, it has to be analyzed many times by different investigators and in different circumstances. The result of any one observation or experiment needs to be confirmed by others in the same country and also in other countries. The validity of a scientific hypothesis is far more severely tested than that of a philosophical principle. Thanks to a vast number of observations, we know that anyone transported from sea level to a high altitude shows symptoms of mountain sickness. After a few weeks, these symptoms disappear; the person has become acclimatized. Examination of the blood then shows that the red corpuscles have greatly multiplied. It is thus legitimate to deduce that the organism adjusts itself to the rarefaction of oxygen in the atmosphere by increasing the quantity of hemoglobin capable of stabilizing this gas. This brings to light many aspects of the law of adaption. Observation of the behavior of men in all epochs and all countries has shown that the human being who is not degenerate seeks at the same time freedom and discipline, activity and repose, adventure and security. This is an inherent characteristic of his nature, a law of his being. Only by observing that nature can we deduce its laws with any certainty since those laws are nothing but the fundamental modes of being, the essential trends and primordial needs of all men in all ages as they appear in the individual, in society and in the race.

Life has so many modes of being that we cannot know them all. We must choose the most primordial and it is easy to go astray in our choice. Thinking matter is far more complex than inert matter. Men's reciprocal relations are less easily defined than those of molecules or atoms. We must be careful not to lose our way among the host of tendencies, needs, appetites and desires we are apt to consider fundamental. Contingent aspects of individual or collective life often appear as necessary: man is easily tempted to think the forms of life which he desires are intended by nature. In the sixteenth century, Bodin was already teaching that the natural law forbids a sovereign to annex his subjects' possessions. The Physiocrats were also presuming that the human world was built according to laws analagous to those of physics. These laws appeared to them precisely the ones which guaranteed economic prosperity. They therefore taught that, in pursuing one's private interest one was, of necessity, working in the interest of all. Adam Smith raised the desire for gain to the dignity of a natural law. Ignorant of scientific method, the eighteenth century economists thought they were able to discover the secret of human relations as easily as the scientists discovered that of the relations of things. Jeremy Bentham imagined himself to be doing for the science of man what Newton had done for the science of matter. The Marxists, even more than the Utilitarians, claimed to use the scientific method in working out their doctrine. But neither Marx, Engels nor Lenin had any experience of scientific research. They ignored the very existence of operational concepts. Unsuspectingly, they mixed up two types of mental discipline; they confused a philosophic interpretation of life with the science of man. Thus Marxism, like Liberalism, put economics before everything else. Such errors show how careful we must be to distinguish which laws of life are really fundamental.

There are, of course, certain characteristics of the individual and the race which are indisputably real and universal. An immediate datum of observation is that everyone in good physical and mental health wants to remain alive. The number of suicides is relatively extremely small. It is equally certain that living creatures are irresistibly driven to reproduce themselves. Nor can one doubt that mind has progressively emerged from living matter in the course of the evolution of the animal species. Equally, in every individual, progressive development of consciousness takes place from the moment of birth to the threshold of old age. From these three orders of phenomena three inseparable, yet distinct, laws naturally follow; those of the conservation of life, the propagation of the race and the development of the mind.   Though these laws are in fact, like philosophical principles, abstractions, they are abstractions very close to the concrete and still impregnated with reality. Though they cannot be expressed in mathematical formulas, they are legitimate children of the scientific method. They are obviously derived from the analysis of the amazingly complex activities of animals and men. We can trust them as surely as we trust the laws of gravity and of the conservation of energy.

3 | *Law of the Preservation of Life.—Its Automatic Aspect.—Its Conscious and Voluntary Aspect.—Exceptions to this Law.—Aberrations of the Instinct of Self-Preservation.*

If life had not an irresistible tendency to preserve itself, it would no longer exist today. The instinct of self-preservation makes the herd panic when the prairie catches fire. The wild animal reacts instinctively against adverse conditions in its environment in such a way as to assure the continuity of its existence. In man this reaction is both automatic and voluntary.

The law of self-preservation is written in the structure of our body and expressed in a very special mode of unconscious activity in our tissues; the adaptive function. To some extent the organism models itself on events; it automatically improvises a manner of facing each new situation. This manner is of such a kind that it tends to make our continuance as long as possible. Confronted with danger, the physical processes always take the direction which leads to the maximum survival of the individual. Thanks to this power of adaptation in all anatomical systems, the onslaughts of the external world, instead of wearing out our organs, strengthen them. Life is preserved and intensified by the struggle against heat, cold, rain, wind and hunger. In the same way, the attacks of bacteria, of other men, of cares and sorrows bring into play conservative mechanisms in our bodies and minds without our being aware of it. They provoke a spontaneous effort in heart, blood vessels, brain, glands and muscles; in fact in all our organs. Warm-blooded animals are so made that the interior environment of the cell tissues must remain invariable. Life can only be preserved on these terms. Since the external environment is essentially variable, the great anatomical systems work full time to neutralize these changes and to maintain the constancy of the internal milieu. The law of adaptation is to the living world what the second law of thermodynamics is to the cosmic. This strange function takes on as many aspects as the various new situations encountered by the tissues and tissue fluids. Not being the specific expression of any organic system, it can be defined only by its purpose. Its means vary: its end remains the same—the conservation of life. The organism fights disease by producing substances which destroy the microbes; against hemorrhages by weakness and sometimes by a momentary stoppage of the heartbeats; against privation of food by diminishing the chemical changes in the tissues; against old age by slowing down the tempo of the physiological rhythm. The spontaneous defense produced by the organism is similar to the resistance opposed by a stable physical system to any factor which tends to modify its equilibrium. If, for example, one dissolves sugar in water, the temperature is lowered and this reduction of heat makes the sugar less soluble. The law of adaptation is as essential to the world of living things as Le Chatelier's principle is to that of physics. It represents the principal mechanism by which life is preserved.

Human beings have become partly conscious of this obstinate attachment to existence. We have an innate fear of death. To us of the West, life appears as the supreme good. Anyone who tries to lay hands on our land, our money or on anything else indispensable to our survival becomes our mortal enemy. To fight an invader has always been considered the noblest of duties. Like the wild animals who devour each other in the jungle, human beings struggle incessantly for self-preservation. The same motive drives the tiger to conquer the prey which prevents it from dying of hunger, and drives civilized man to conquer markets and acquire raw materials. The fight for survival demands incessant activity of body and mind. Life can only be preserved and increased by effort. We recoil from no effort, however painful, when it is a question of surviving. Even when life is a torment, we still try to hold on to it. To keep alive man will consent to be the slave of a machine or to do stultifying work in an office. He will not shrink from the long sufferings of poverty, from dishonorable flight from the enemy, from the infirmities of old age or from the hopeless struggle against incurable disease. The very structure of our body and of our consciousness imposes on us as a primary duty the obligation to maintain life.

This tendency of life to conserve itself seems less irresistible in its conscious aspect than in its unconscious. Intelligence and will do not watch over our existence as unremittingly as does the automatism of the adaptive systems. The great sympathetic nervous system is a more vigilant guardian of the organism than the brain is. Man is the only animal who occasionally prefers death to life. He commits suicide or acquires habits of living which are equivalent to suicide. In all epochs of history man has considered it an honor to die in battle. His behavior is not invariably inspired by the principle of self-preservation.

Man is, as we know, free to violate every natural law. He is guided not by instinct but by intelligence, and intelligence is fallible. By an effort of will, he can control even his deepest impulses. He can silence even the call of life itself. When life ceases to have any value for him, he kills himself. He destroys, in fact, what is already dead.

Stranger still, civilized beings have established customs which render life itself impossible, such as the herding together of people in industrial towns, the suppression of natural modes of existence, excessive drinking and the throwing off of all moral restraint. But these errors are mainly due to ignorance of the conditions life exacts, for Western man has a mania to live. This frenzy can be measured by the enormous efforts he makes to avoid dying. Though he does not realize that many modern habits weaken and destroy human beings, he realizes the immense usefulness of hygiene and medicine and has made every effort to develop these sciences. Everywhere, research laboratories have been built at great expense to further our knowledge of chemistry, bacteriology, and physiology; everywhere great medical schools are being set up. New York is dominated by the vast buildings of the Medical Center of Columbia University while on the bank of the East River there looms the huge mass of the Rockefeller Institute.

4 | *The Law of the Propagation of the Race.—Sexual Attraction.—Mother Love.—Their Organic Bases.—Dissociation of the Sexual Act and Impregnation.*

All animals have a second fundamental tendency which is no less imperious than that of the preservation of life. All living creatures are irresistibly driven to reproduce themselves. Man is the only animal who can oppose the barrier of his will against the unleashing of his sexual appetite. There have been ascetics in all ages but they have always been few for, after hunger and thirst, the sexual appetite is the most urgent of all. Nature sets almost as much importance on the propagation of life as on its preservation. She strikes those whom she is scheming to join together with a kind of madness. The substances liberated in the blood by the testicles or the ovaries act so powerfully on the brain

centers that clarity of judgment is obscured. Sexual desire is
the undisputed master of individuals and of nations. The
history of peoples, like that of families, frequently depends
on the genetic caprices of its rulers. Vast numbers of men
have sacrificed fortune or honor in obedience to the impulse
of their genital glands. The need to propagate the race can
at moments dominate the need to preserve life; love is literally stronger than death. We must not confuse love with
genetic desire. Love surpasses desire as much as a conflagra-
tion surpasses the flame of a match. It is a product, still some-
what mysterious to us, of the ductless glands, the nerve
centers and the mind. It causes one human being to give
himself for ever to another human being. It forges an indestructible coupling between male and female; it completes
the union of bodies by the union of souls. It assures permanence, peace and happiness in the family; three things which
are indispensable to the best development of man's offspring.
It constitutes the subtlest and most impressive of the processes employed by nature to ensure the propagation of the race
and the raising of the individual to his highest level.

In the handing on of life, the female plays a far more
important part than the male. It is in the tissues and in the
soul of woman that we can decipher the purposes of the law
of the propagation of the race. Females of all species have
an almost sacred respect for their young. Mother love goes
far deeper than sexual love. The bitch, like the lioness, de-
fends her litter with reckless courage. Woman, when she is
not degenerate, does not hesitate to give her life for her
children. Unconsciously she follows the law written in her
flesh and blood since before the dawn of humanity. Nature
prefers the child to the mother. At the outset of the famine
in Madrid, the women grew lean, but still bore children of
normal weight. But, as the quantity of food had been too
little to satisfy the needs of both mother and fetus, the fetus

had grown at the mother's expense. So too, the mother's milk hardly varied in quality and quantity. The baby flourished but the nursing mother lost a quarter of her weight during the period of lactation. Thus the mother was automatically sacrificed to the child.

In other circumstances sacrifice, instead of being unconscious, becomes voluntary. Parents usually prefer the wellbeing of their children to their own. During the famine in Paris many parents and grandparents went without food in favor of the young and sometimes died as the result.

In dogs, maternal love only lasts for a short time; in monkeys it persists much longer. In the human species, it never ceases, for man's progeny need love and their mother needs to love. However long they live, however humble their position, parents who have suceeded in bringing up satisfactory children feel, in their last moments, that they have fully accomplished their destiny. In the sickness or infirmity of old age they are rewarded by the serene joy which nature grants to those who have obeyed her completely.

Men and women are different from each other but complementary. They are particularized by far more than their genital organs and their physical conformation. Their cells, their body fluids and even their blood carry the anatomical or chemical imprint of their sex. It is literally in the very depths of the tissues that the individual's destiny of propagating his species is inscribed. The genetic impulse which appears at puberty comes under the influence of unknown causes, of the mysterious ductless glands.

The pituitary body, this little group of glandular cells which is partly enclosed in the base of the skull, lets loose certain very active substances into the blood. These substances are carried by the blood stream to the testicles or the ovaries and condition their functioning. The suprarenal and thyroid glands also contribute to genital activity. At the moment of puberty they determine the appearance of the specific characteristics of either sex. It is evident that the organism is entirely regulated with reference to the sexual function and hence to the propagation of life. Woman is far more specifically designed for this part than man. Her organic and psychic functions are centered on the cyclic changes of the ovary. *Tota mulier in utero,* said the ancients. The manufacture of the ovules, the preparation for eventual motherhood, pregnancy and suckling are woman's natural destiny. If she eludes this destiny, danger awaits her. Lack of physical and mental balance is the price woman has to pay when living conditions or her own will prevent her from fulfilling her natural function. Mother love is not a virtue; it is a function of the feminine nervous system as mother's milk is a secretion of the mammary glands. Both depend on the same substance—prolactine, which is set loose in the blood by the posterior lobe of the pituitary body. This gland, through its action on the genital organs, the breasts and the brain, directs both the impulses which lead to copulation and those which give a woman the love for her child and the possibility of suckling it.

The progress of contraceptive methods has dissociated the sexual act from impregnation. At the same time, abortion has ceased to be considered a crime. Both man and woman have left off obeying the law of the propagation of the race. At first nature remained silent. The transgressors themselves were punished lightly or not at all. Then came fearful catastrophes. France has declined, England is following suit and a great qualitative change is taking place in the United States. The severity of the punishment proves how grave was the fault.

Yet even for the moderns, the need to propagate the race remains as fundamental as the need to conserve life. It is rooted in our physical and mental structure; our whole organism is permeated with sexuality. The glands which produce the elements of the future being are also those which give strength and courage to his parent. To propagate life is both a primordial urge and an essential need.

> *Law of the Ascendance of Mind in the Course of*
> 5 *Evolution of Animals and Human Beings.—The Development of the Brain and the Coming of Intelligence.*

Life has a third tendency, much less easy to verify but just as fundamental as the other two. This is the upward trend of mind in the course of the evolution of living creatures. Paleontology, like history, is only a conjectural science. Its data are few and often highly uncertain. Since it is far from possessing the precision of chemistry or physics, we cannot hope that it will give us an exact knowledge of our forefathers. Nevertheless it offers us documents of undoubted value about our past. Considered in broad outline, the evolution of living things is an established fact. Mind only manifested itself as distinct from matter after a long ascent through the animal forms which succeeded each other, from the amoeba to man, on the surface of our planet.

Perhaps it was already present on earth before the appearance of life. Perhaps it was already implicit in the creative idea which was progressively realized in unicellular creatures, invertebrates, fish, amphibians, reptiles and finally warm-blooded animals. Claude Bernard wrote: "The governing idea of this vital evolution belongs essentially to the realm of life and not to chemistry, physics or anything else." In this aspect plants and trees resemble animals. Is there not a creative idea in the acorn which develops little by little and manifests itself fully in the oak? It seems that the development of the species, like that of the individual, comes about through the impetus of an immanent force which has some analogy with thought. But this thought is very different from human thought, being at once blind and clear-sighted, lavish and thrifty, hesitant and assured. Mind was incapable of manifesting itself in the world under the aspect we know it today until living matter had acquired an appropriate structure. The realization of this structure demanded a preparation which lasted perhaps a thousand million years. Then, side by side with the gigantic and stupid dinosaurs with their rudimentary brain, appeared small, intelligent, alert animals whose blood had a constant temperature. The rapid progress of cerebral matter began with the first mammals, probably forty to fifty million years ago. This was an immensely significant event, for a certain degree of perfection of this brain substance was indispensable to the appearance of mind in living matter. Paleontology gives us a very incomplete picture of our history. The documents on which the doctrine of evolution is based are few in number. It is possible that the missing links in the chain will never be brought to light by new discoveries.

Perhaps even the proofs of our descent from an ancestor whom we have in common with the anthropoid apes do not exist. Nevertheless, it is certain that the brain was perfected irregularly, discontinuously but progressively through the animal series over millions of years. From the rudimentary aspect it presented in the lower animals such as the medusa, the nervous system arrived at extreme complexity in the mammal. It was particularly complex in the tarsier which some paleontologists consider as our probable ancestor. The brains of the marmoset, the monkey and the anthropoid ape show an enlargement in the centers of sight, touch and the movements of the extremities. Though the relations between the brain and the mind are far from being fully known, we do know that mind depends on the quantity and quality of the substance of the brain and on the endocrine glands. It is also certain that intelligence does not depend only on the volume of the brain, for the brain of some idiots is as large as that of Napoleon. Relative to its own weight, the mouse possesses a brain heavier than man's, yet the mouse is not more intelligent. On the other hand the volume of the nervous substance in reptiles, dinosaurs and birds was small in comparison with that of the other tissues. It becomes much greater in mammals and above all in primates. In spite of the gropings, the stops and the sudden leaps of evolution, brain and intelligence continued to develop simultaneously.

During the Miocene period, perhaps twenty or thirty million years ago, there were already great anthropoids in the forests of Europe whose cranial capacity was no less than that of gorillas existing today. The brain of a gorilla weighing more than 300 kilograms does not exceed 600 cubic centimeters. At the end of the Pliocene period appeared a phenomenon of immense importance. This was the rapid growth of the brain in creatures which in some ways resembled the anthropoid of the Miocene period. One of the first creatures whose cerebral volume was clearly superior to that of the other primates lived in Java, possibly five hundred thousand years ago. This was Pithecanthropus, whose cranial capacity was roughly 900 centimeters and whose facial angle was 52 degrees. Some hundreds of thousands of years before him there was, in Sussex, a still more intelligent being; the Ecanthropus of Piltdown whose cerebral volume was nearly 1,350 cubic centimeters. This creature could already roughly fashion flint into tools and weapons. It was probably about the same time that the Sinanthropus, or man of Peiping, flourished. Much later, after the fourth ice age, perhaps forty thousand to one hundred thousand years before the Christian era, appeared Neanderthal man. This stocky little creature, with its short, powerful neck, still had the appearance of an anthropoid. He lived in Germany, near Düsseldorf, and also in the valley of the Dordogne in France. He manufactured very beautiful flint tools. His facial angle varied from 58 degrees to 67 degrees. His cranial capacity, about 1,550 cubic centimeters, equaled that of the present inhabitants of Europe. About twenty or thirty thousand years ago, he gave place, as we know, to Cro-Magnon man whose highest facial angle was 65 degrees and whose powers of observation, aesthetic sense and manual skill were probably not inferior to own own.

Mind arose slowly through a series of animal forms in the course of hundreds of millions of years. Then, hardly two thousand centuries ago, from the beginning of the Pleistocene era, this rise was greatly accelerated. In spite of geological convulsions, repeated freezing of the earth's surface, attacks of formidable prehistoric animals, famine and disease, man automatically continued his journey toward the light. He made weapons and tools; he discovered fire; he invented the wheel; he cultivated grain; he domesticated wild animals. And, when his intelligence and his inventions had procured him some leisure, he began to reflect on the nature of things, of himself, of the universe and of God. In the fortieth century B.C., the Egyptians already possessed a written code of morals. According to the Canon of Confucius, the Chinese astronomers of the twenty-fourth century determined the summer and winter solstices and approximately calculated the length of the year. A century later, the Emperor Shun offered prayers and sacrifices to a single God. Finally, in the sixth century, with the philosophers of the Ionian School, Thales, Anaximander and Anaximenes, came the dawn of our own civilization.

Thus, over a space of time no longer in the history of liv-

ing beings than one hour in the life of a man, mind emerged
from matter and installed itself on our planet. From that
moment it continued its ascent in two distinct, though complementary directions. It took the road of intellect, the
creator of philosophy and science, and the road of feeling,
that is to say of art, religion and morality.

6 | *Development of Intellect and Feeling in the Race.*

Intellect chose to take its first great flight from the tiny
promontory which Asia sends out into the Atlantic ocean
to the north of the Mediterranean. With one beat of its
wings it rose, in ancient Greece, to a height it has hardly
surpassed today. From the very first it attacked redoubtable
problems; problems which succeeding philosophers from
Pythagoras, Plato and Socrates to Kant and Bergson have not
yet been capable of solving. But the intellect did not rest
content with philosophy. From Greece it emigrated to the
west of Europe where, in a flight of genius, it created science. Then its success became prodigious. During the short
time which separates the age of Galileo and of Newton from
that of Claude Bernard, Pasteur and Planck, it discovered
the essential laws of the inanimate and the animate world.
Thanks to it, "men obtained the mastery of everything on
the face of the earth except themselves."

Feeling, under the form of art, poetry, moral greatness,
religious inspiration, has been the light of humanity since
the dawn of prehistoric times. As soon as it emerged from
original night, the mind attempted to reproduce the beauty
of things in wood, ivory or stone and to express it in music
and poetry. There had been unknown artists in the Cro-
Magnon era. Later there had been Phidias, Praxiteles and

Virgil. At the same time the mind had been aspiring to the idea of moral beauty, of truth and of God. It had raised up Plato, Aristotle, Zeno and Epictetus. Then, suddenly, it took a tremendous flight.

. . In an unknown village of Palestine, on the shores of Lake Tiberias, a young carpenter announced some astonishing news to a few ignorant fishermen. We are loved by an immaterial and all-powerful Being. This Being is accessible to our prayers. We must love Him above all creatures. And we ourselves must also love one another.

A new era had begun. The only cement strong enough to bind men together had been found. Nevertheless, humanity chose to ignore the importance of this new principle in the organization of its collective life. It is far from having understood that only mutual love could save it from division, ruin and chaos. Nor has it realized that no scientific discovery was so fraught with significance as the revelation of the law of love by Jesus the Crucified. For this law is, in fact, that of the survival of human societies.

Only in individual life was the evangelical law applied to a certain extent. Although man still had in the depths of his nature the savage and lustful appetites of the gorilla, he felt the beauty of charity and renunciation. He was drawn to the heroism which, in the hell of modern warfare, consists in giving one's life for one's friends; and in having pity on the vanquished, the sick, the weak and the abandoned. This need for sacrifice and brotherhood became more defined in the course of centuries. Then appeared St. Louis of France, St. Francis of Assisi, St. Vincent de Paul and a numberless legion of apostles of charity.

Even in our own base and egotistical age, thousands of men and women still follow, on the battlefield, in the monastery or in that abomination of desolation the modern city, the path of heroism, abnegation and holiness.

At the same time a still bolder and more astonishing aim came to be specified. This was to attain awareness of the unknown realm which extends beyond science and philosophy: the realm on whose threshold the intellect automatically comes to a standstill. Inspired souls such as St. Benedict, St. John of the Cross, Eckhardt and Ruysbroek taught men in the West how they could attain God by following the path of asceticism and mysticism. They taught them in other words, how to satisfy the age-old desire of the human soul to unite itself to this Being immanent in all things who, instead of being coextensive with nature like the Wisdom of Heraclitus, dominates it like Jehovah and, like the God of St. Francis of Assisi, has a father's love for us.

Our civilization has, in truth, forgotten that it is born of the blood of Christ; it has also forgotten God. But it still understands the beauty of the Gospel narratives and of the Sermon on the Mount. It is still moved by those words of pity and love which bring peace, and sometimes even joy, to the broken, the afflicted, the sick and the dying; to all of us who will sooner or later be crushed by the pitiless mechanisms of life.

Today, in spite of the failure of ideologies and universal confusion, intellect and feeling continue their soaring flight. True, humanity leaves behind it an innumerable crowd of the mediocre and the feeble-minded, of moral imbeciles, madmen, criminals, and degenerates of all types. Nevertheless, it does not cease to engender people of greater and greater mental power. Are not the rulers, heroes, scholars and saints produced by modern civilization superior to Pericles, Caesar and all the great men of antiquity? Although the brain has not measurably increased its volume since the Neanderthal era, i.e. for more than four hundred centuries, its functional value has been immensely enhanced. This may be the result of qualitative changes in the nervous cells or in the secretions of the glandular cells which, mingled with the blood, steep the brain; modifications which our histological and chemical techniques cannot yet reveal. Perhaps it is simply due to the handing on of accumulated knowledge and to better living conditions. Whatever the reason, mental power is gradually increasing in the race in spite of the unworthiness of the majority of individuals.

The emergence of mind from matter very likely constitutes the whole point of evolution and the most important event in the history of the universe. On all the evidence, this sudden rise of consciousness in living forms is the expression of a fundamental mode of life.

7 | *Law of the Ascent of Mind in the Course of the Evolution of the Individual.—Character at Once Automatic and Voluntary of the Development of Consciousness.*

Consciousness appears at a particular moment in the evolution of the individual as in that of the race. This emergence of the spiritual beyond the material, beyond the mass of cells and blood which make up the organism, is an immediate datum of observation. It constitutes an essential character of the substance of which we are made. Human life begins in the night of the spirit. The ovule, even when it potentially contains the genius of Newton, Goethe or Napoleon, differs little from those unicellular creatures which during the Archeozoic period of the Precambrian age, represented the humble beginning of living things on the earth's surface. Once fertilized, the ovule divides and engenders the embryo; the embryo becomes the fetus; the child is born. But the night continues until those wonderful moments in the first year when the mother sees the dawn of intelligence arise in her baby's eyes. Like morning light in the tropics, intelligence grows fast. In a few dozen months, a human child journeys the whole road which it took living forms perhaps more than a thousand million years to traverse in their ascent toward mind. From the mental, as well as from the bodily point of view, the evolution of the individual presents some analogy, as Haechel supposed, with the evolution of the species. The phylogenic evolution of mind appears to prefigure the ontogenic.

Mental development is at once automatic and voluntary. In infancy it is entirely automatic, as in the development of organs, muscles and bones. It is only later that it asks help from the intelligence and the will. At first the mind grows, along with the nervous system and the other tissues, under the internal impulse of the hereditary forces which have their seat in the genes of all the cells of the organism. It is the influence of the genes which gives it, like the features of our face, a certain likeness to our parents or to certain of our ancestors. Nevertheless, the actualization of inherited potentialities is not inevitable. It depends on the physical and chemical conditions of the environment in which the individual develops. This is why many individuals remain inferior all their life to what they might have been. The soul is not independent of the body; the quality of the mind depends on that of the organs, particularly that of the brain and the endocrine glands. No microcephalous genius has ever appeared. If Virgil had been the victom of thyroidal myxedema or of pancreatic diabetes, he would not have written the Aeneid. It is true, however, that the great soul can inhabit a sickly body. Sometimes disease is not incompatible with a highly elevated mind; St. Thérèse of Lisieux was tubercular. Syphilis, on the contrary, often injures the brain but sometimes gives a splendid richness to thought. Alphonse Daudet suffered from locomotor ataxia; Guy de Maupassant died of general paralysis. There are organic defects which attack the soul and others which leave it undamaged. But the state of consciousness is never wholly independent of the state of the tissues, body fluids and blood.

The spontaneous growth of the mind always remains incomplete. Man can only give full play to his mind by the effort of his own will. One cannot become an athlete without training. In the same way one has to work hard to increase one's powers of awareness. If a pupil has no will to learn, the most brilliant schoolmaster can teach him nothing. Reading moral treatises will not make us virtuous. Only we ourselves can forge our own souls.

The formation of personality is equivalent, to use Bergson's expression, to the creation of the self by the self. This creation of the self by the self consists in drawing from our body and our consciousness more than they contain; in modeling our interior life according to an ideal. We have to construct in ourselves, with the help of materials which may often be mediocre, a new and powerful spirit. This miracle occurs every day in the history of mankind. Great men often arise from the humblest origins. But all, ignorant and learned, rich and poor, young and old, are equally capable, if they are really determined, of releasing the hidden spiritual energy in their own depths. Though consciousness develops side by side with the body it does not stop developing when the body has finished growing.

| 8 | *Development of Intellect and Feeling in the Individual.—The Secret of Life.—The End of the Ascent.— The Great Refusal.* |

It is in middle age, when physiological activities have become less intense, that consciousness tends to become deeper, wider, more purified. Intellect, esthetic activity, moral strength and the religious sense continue to develop even in old age. It was when Dante was complaining of decrepitude that he wrote the most sublime lines of the *Paradiso.* But it is only in those who have served it faithfully all their lives that spirit continues to soar till the very end.

Most men do not realize that they are the makers of their spiritual destiny. Furthermore, they take no heed of this destiny. We know already that the development of mind in the individual is far from being inevitable as it has been in the race. In the course of the evolution of innumerable animal species, consciousness has hesitated, groped about and come up against a barrier which has permanently arrested it. This has happened, for example, in the case of ants and bees. It often happens in the same way in the individual. Consciousness cannot achieve its finest development without education and effort of will. By a strange aberration civilized man is not concerned about the progress of his soul. A large section of the population never advances beyond the psychological age of twelve or thirteen. We do not know the exact causes of this disastrous arrested development. Generally speaking, mental infantilism is to be observed in the descendants of drunkards, syphilitics, and mental and moral defectives. However, it is not always hereditary; it can be due to defective nutrition, to the action of toxic substances,

to bad physical habits or to the attacks of certain viruses.
Among those whose intelligence develops further, many are
still incapable of attaining full mental maturity. These could,
nevertheless, use the leisure given them by the progress of
machinery to improve themselves both physically and spiritually.

Instead of doing so, they waste their free time in drinking, card-playing, going to the movies or the dance hall or
reading novels on their own mental level. They are victims
at once of their education and of the habits of modern life.

Nevertheless, the defects of our time do not invalidate
the law of the development of the mind and spirit. The
existence of disease does not imply that health is an illusion.
In all ages the most highly evolved human beings have applied their will to improve their minds. Unfortunately, in
modern society this effort is ill-directed; it has divorced
intellect from feeling. Frequently it creates the desire for
knowledge and the powers of observation, criticism, imagination and discovery but hardly ever does it deal with the
nonintellectual activities of the human spirit. It neglects
almost entirely such things as courage, audacity, self-sacrifice, heroism and love.

Maeterlinck once wrote: "To see without loving is to stare
into darkness." By its emphasis on the exclusive development
of reason, modern education arrests the development of the
spirit. The preparation for nearly every examination forms
the memory without forming the intelligence and, moreover, its spiritual value is null. Nevertheless, the interest of
the community demands a profound intellectual culture. We
need engineers, historians, physicists, mathematicians and
philosophers. Only intellectual specialists are capable of advancing knowledge. Specialization is a necessary evil but its
penalty is the narrowing of the spirit. The atmosphere of
libraries, lecture rooms and laboratories is dangerous to

those who shut themselves up in them too long. It separates us from reality like a fog. Without Gretchen, Faust would never have realized that the secret of life is not to be found in books.

The secret of life is to be found in life itself; in the full organic, intellectual and spiritual activities of our body. This secret can never be discovered by considering any of these three orders of activity in isolation. When the spirit rises in us under the impulse of will, like the sap in the tree under the impulse of spring, it appears simultaneously as intelligence, judgment, self-mastery and moral beauty. It becomes that intellectual light brimming with love of which Dante speaks in the *Paradiso*. It is wisdom; that wisdom which is refused to abstract philosophers and scientists. For scientists and philosophers consider things which cannot be expressed in words as unreal. Neither Jean-Jacques Rousseau, Auguste Comte nor Claude Bernard were truly wise. It is often among the anonymous and humble that one meets the true elect of the spirit. In other days they were to be found among the men and women who tilled their fields along with their children and servants; also among that small rural aristocracy who lived almost like peasants. This luminous yet inarticulate wisdom still exists in some rural families, in certain old country doctors, in humble priests and in unknown heroes of selflessness and charity. Yet it has also been found in emperors and kings. Was the spirit of Marcus Aurelius or St. Louis less noble than that of Socrates or Epictetus? The path which leads to the mountain summit is equally rough and magnificent for all. There is no spiritual ascent without sacrifice: sacrifice of fortune or reputation; sacrifice of life for love of one's friends, one's country or a great ideal. It is implicit in the soldier who goes willingly into the horrors of a modern battle; in Noguchi, frail, alone and ill, leaving his laboratory in the Rockefeller Institute to go and die of yellow fever in Africa; in those who have a passion for beauty and truth, who reach out with all their strength toward God, who give their lives that justice and love may reign on earth. It is not reason but feeling which leads man to the height of his destiny. The spirit rises by suffering and desire rather than by intellect; at a certain point of the journey it leaves the intellect, whose weight is too heavy, behind it. It reduces itself to the essence of the soul which is love. Alone, in the midst of this dark night of the reason, it escapes from time and space and, by a process which the great mystics themselves have never been able to describe, it unites itself to the ineffable substratum of all things. Perhaps this union with God is the secret goal toward which the individual strives from the moment when the fertilized ovule begins its division and growth in the mother's womb.

Only a very few people achieve spiritual evolution for it demands a persistent effort of will, a certain state of the tissues, a sense of the heroic and a purification of the senses and the mind. It also demands other conditions which we only dimly understand; in particular that psychophysiological condition which the Church calls Grace. But all can set out on this path which, though it must be followed through clouds, leads to the radiance of the heights. We can also, if we choose, instead of obeying the governing idea of individual evolution, live only for the satisfaction of our physical appetites, like our cousins the apes. Most civilized people are still so near the animal kingdom that they are only occupied with material values. Actually their existence is far lower than that of the animals for only spiritual values can bring us light and joy. At a given moment of his life everyone must choose between the material and the human. He must refuse or accept obedience to the law of the development of the spirit. It is just as dangerous to remain undecided as to refuse altogether. "Because thou art neither hot nor cold I will spew thee out of my mouth," it is written in the Apocalypse. Though, in most people, consciousness arrests its development early, its natural tendency is to grow steadily from birth to death. The uprising of the spirit in the course of the evolution of every individual is more·than a fundamental law of human life; it is its distinctive characteristic.

> 9 | *Fundamental Unity of the Laws of Life.—Their Hierarchy.—Specifically Human Character of the Law of Spiritual Ascent.*

It is thus a definite datum of observation that life tends to conserve itself, to reproduce itself and to spiritualize itself. The laws of conservation and reproduction are as old as life itself. Their existence is evident in the most rudimentary animal forms. This is not true of the law of spiritual development. This fundamental tendency may have been latent in unicellular living creatures but it did not manifest itself in the race and in the individual until a much later stage of evolution; at the moment of the appearance of the mammals, the primates and above all of man. It constitutes in truth our specific character, for man, alone of all the animals, is able to contribute to the development of the personality by voluntary effort.

The three fundamentals laws of our life constitute different aspects of one and the same thing. Similarly, man's multiple activities are only facets of his unity. Heart, lungs, brain and endocrine glands have no autonomous existence: these organs are inseparable from each other and inseparable from the whole organism. No single one of our natural tendencies can be considered in isolation; each is essential just as each organ is essential. It is impossible to do without the kidneys, the thyroid gland, the heart or the pancreas: it is equally impossible to disobey any one of the capital obligations of living beings. Undoubtedly we are free to obey only one or two of these laws or even to reject all three but only lunatics take this last course. Yet many normal and even eminently intelligent individuals consider it clever or meritorious to obey only such natural tendencies as they find agreeable. Some concentrate all their efforts on self-preservation; these constitute the dregs of humanity; others both preserve and propagate life; they themselves remain submen but the spirit may spring up at any moment among their descendants. Others sacrifice the reproduction and even the preservation of life to follow exclusively their spiritual or imaginative impulses. This group is composed at once of egoists and heroes, of sages and madmen. But life takes no account of the intentions of those who disobey her. She punishes the sage and the hero just as much as the self-centered, the ignorant and the mad. She strikes them or their nation with decadence. The only virtue which exists for her is obedience to her threefold law. This virtue she royally rewards by granting happiness to those who acquire it.

Modern society has committed the fundamental error of disobeying the law of spiritual development. It has arbitrarily reduced spirit to mere intellect. It has cultivated the intellect because, thanks to science, the intellect gives it mastery of the physical world. But it has ignored those other activities of the spirit which can never be more than partially represented in scientific language and which are only expressed in action, art and prayer. Our schools do not teach self-discipline, order, good manners or courage. The school curriculum does not give children sufficient contact either with the beauty of things or the beauty of art. Finally, our schools have forgotten that all ancient civilizations at the height of their greatness had a strong sense of religion. They have forgotten that the soul of Western civilization was steeped in Christianity from its infancy and that nothing has replaced the beauty and purity of the evangelical morality in men's hearts. This ignorance provokes a slow and smothered protest from life, particularly marked in villages and small towns. There is a rising tide of ugliness, dirt, grossness and drunkenness. Along with a passion for comfort and security we find envy, calumny and mutual hate; we find, too, the vices which Dante considered the most abject of all: hypocrisy, lying and treachery. Life has responded automatically to the refusal to conform to the law of spiritual development by becoming degraded and degenerate. Intellectual and moral development are both equally necessary but moral atrophy brings on us more irremediable disasters.

Though the laws of life are inseparable, they form a natural hierarchy. The principles of conservation and reproduction are the oldest and determine our most irresistible impulses. The law of spiritual development is of far more recent origin and is indeed a very new tendency of life. In many people it is still so weak and hesitating as to be hardly perceptible. Conflicts between the primordial needs often arise in the depths of consciousness. Sometimes we have to choose between preserving our existence and propagating the race: sometimes between serving the spirit or serving life. The choice is always difficult and often impossible. Up to what point should a woman risk her life in order to propagate the race? Do tuberculosis of the lungs, heart disease or other disabilities dispense her from the duty of motherhood? Far more conflicts arise between the law of spiritual ascent and the laws of self-preservation and reproduction. Today, as in all ages, men and women still renounce parenthood to devote themselves to the care of others or to a religious ideal. Many, too, sacrifice their lives for what they believe. Each one of these suffers an inner conflict of varying degrees of violence between commandments which all, generally speaking, demand to be obeyed. In the noblest, the struggle always ends in submission to that law of life which is peculiar to man. Socrates drank the hemlock; St. Paul was beheaded; Joan of Arc was burnt at the stake. Each time the whole level of humanity was raised. Today it is the heroes and the martyrs who advance life further along that mysterious way on which it set out from its beginning in the abyss of time.

CHAPTER FOUR

Good and Evil

	Uncertainty of the Notion of Good and Evil.—Neces-
1	*sity for a single Definition.—Good and Evil Are De-*
	termined by the Structure of Human Life.

In no time and in no country have moralists agreed on the definition of good and evil. Some have identified good with the useful, the true, the advantageous or the pleasant. Others have seen it as that which conforms with nature or with the will of God. As to evil, it has been equated with suffering, injustice and ignorance or put down to the prompting of Satan.

Thus the notions of good and evil have always remained various and uncertain. Pleasure is the only good and pain the only evil, said Aristippus of Cyrene. True good has nothing to do with pleasure, answered the Stoics; it resides in knowledge of the order of things and springs from reason. In order to survive, we must ourselves conform to nature and the whole of nature is steeped in God. In Epictetus and Marcus Aurelius the notion of good was confused with that of brotherly love, resignation and submission to the divine will. For the Jews, and later for the Christians, it had a far more definite meaning. The commandments given by God

91

Himself were laid down in the sacred books of the Old and New Testaments. Thus the moralist, like a lawyer interpreting the legal code, could determine without difficulty what was good and what was evil. In principle it was this idea of the lawful and the forbidden which governed the conduct of men in the West up to the end of the Middle Ages. Nevertheless, the morality of pleasure continued its career unperturbed through the centuries. Rejuvenated by Helvetius and Jeremy Bentham, it became the morality of self-interest. Its success then became overwhelming for man is always ready to take egoism as his supreme guiding principle. In modern democracies, the good became definitely identified with the useful. Egoism proved itself stronger than love. Epicurus vanquished Christ.

Only a very small minority still accepts the definition of good and evil traditional in Western civilization. The majority have forgotten the Ten Commandments; many even ignore their very existence. There is no longer any universally recognized frontier between licit and illicit. Most people do not distinguish clearly between good and evil. They are not even capable of taking enlightened selfishness as the arbiter of their actions. They are content to obey their appetites and to pursue their immediate advantage. Good is merely profit. Since courage exposes one to useless dangers, it is better to be a coward than a corpse. A motorcar is preferable to a child. The great thing is to earn as much as possible while working the bare minimum. Nevertheless, honesty, loyalty, disinterestedness and heroism are still preached.

Thus there is immense confusion in the mind of modern man. Obviously, the members of human communities should learn to behave according to identical principles. They ought to accept a single definition of good and evil as they accept a single definition of heat and cold.

Such a definition is possible today in the light of the fundamental laws of human life. The lawful can be distinguished from the forbidden with complete certainty. The knowledge of these laws enables us to define good and evil clearly and unalterably and in a way that is intelligible to every individual endowed with reason. Good consists in what conforms to the essential tendencies of our nature. It comprises those things, thoughts, feelings and acts which tend to conserve life, to propagate the race, to heighten the mental perception of the individual and to raise the spiritual level of mankind. Evil, on the contrary, is that which is opposed to life, to its multiplication or to its spiritual development. The supreme good, in fact, is indistinguishable from the success of life in its specifically human aspect.

When it comes to the triumph of the spirit, good and evil assume a certain complexity. They include not only factors which help or hinder life, considered as a whole or in one of its aspects, but also those which produce harmony or disharmony in our physical and mental activities.

There are things which are evidently bad because they kill, paralyze, corrupt or diminish the individual. Such things, for example, are the plague bacillus, the yellow fever virus, alcoholic excesses, tuberculosis, the movies and the radio. Equally bad are the exclusive development of the intellect at the expense of physical robustness, of the tolerance of dirt, discourtesy and the habit of denigration. Other evils are lack of self-mastery, incapacity for effort and the spirit of deceit. On the contrary, air, water, light, science, art and religion represent essential aspects of good as do the capacities for love, zeal and action. For all these factors make for the heightening of personal and social life.

| 2 | *Definition of Sin.—Reality of Vice and Virtue.—Moral Responsibility.—Old and New Sins.* |

Sin is the refusal to submit to the order of things. Any act or thought which tends to diminish, disintegrate or destroy life in its specifically human expression is a sin. It is a sin to hate one's neighbor, for hate is destructive both of body and spirit. Vice is the result of habitual sin. As to virtue, it does not consist only, as Socrates taught, in the knowledge of good; it is an act of the will, a habit which increases the quantity, intensity, and quality of life. It builds up, strengthens and vivifies personality. Hope, faith, enthusiasm and the will to succeed act on the body like steam on a turbine. Physical and mental activities are purified by love. These virtues heighten the personality and make it stronger and more closely knit. Vice, on the contrary, lessens and disintegrates it: laziness, vacillation, self-pity and melancholy arrest mental development. As to pride, egoism and jealousy, they separate those who are guilty of them from their fellows and dry up the springs of the spirit in themselves. Sexual excesses, gluttony and drunkenness attack the spirit at its source by causing disorders in the body.

In communal life there are social virtues and antisocial vices. Courtesy, cleanliness, love of one's native land, common ideals and a common religion make a society strong and harmonious. Antisocial vices such as rudeness, backbiting and mutual detestation sow discord among members of the same family or social group and eventually bring a nation to impotence and destruction.

Sin appeared in the world at the moment when man, freed from the automatism of instinct, became capable of error. Sin can be voluntary or involuntary. It can result from ig-

norance of the laws of life, from inability to obey them or
from the refusal to conform to the order of things. To what
extent is any given man morally responsible for any given
act? We do not know.

No one can explore the brain, organs and mind of his
neighbor to discover the cause of his actions. The judge
himself, being only a man, is incapable of plumbing the
souls of other men. He must give up trying, even with the
help of the psychiatrists, to find out whether an accused
man is or is not morally responsible for his conduct. He
must be content with deciding whether the man in the dock
is really the author of the crime. Rage, drunkenness, weak-
mindedness or madness should not be any excuse for the
criminal. Whether the aggressor is a drunkard, a lunatic or a
gangster, he has, none the less, victimized someone. The
damage suffered by that victim is not lessened by the moral
irresponsibility of the offender. Society is not qualified to
punish its members, but it has the duty of protecting them.
It should put those who are a danger to the existence of
their neighbors or to their material or spiritual progress in a
position where they can do no further harm. Legislation
needs to be revolutionized. If the drunken motorist who kills
a pedestrian risked the death penalty, drunkenness would
soon appear as something to be avoided. The majority of sins,
whether voluntary or involuntary, which an individual commits damage not only himself but his neighbors. Why does
society not protect its members against slanderers, drunkards
and the mentally unbalanced as it protects them against the
germs of typhoid fever or cholera?

Sins are classified on a scale of gravity which has changed
arbitrarily in different ages. Nevertheless, the seven deadly
sins recognized by the Church continue to deserve first place
in the hierarchy of human disorders. Perhaps we have un-
derestimated the seriousness of some of these for the conse-

quences of certain vices do not appear till after many years
and sometimes after many generations. It is only now, for
example, that we realize what part alcoholism, egoism and
envy play in the degeneration of a people. Side by side with
such ancient sins as pride, jealousy and intemperance there
has been a growth of new and very grievous sins. Our greater
knowledge of natural laws teaches us to appreciate the importance of faults which once seemed negligible. Wrong nutrition can cause incurable defects of body and mind in a
child. Therefore parents who do not take the trouble to learn
how to look after their children properly commit a grave sin.
We know nowadays that marriage between first cousins,
drunkards, syphilitics or carriers of hereditary mental taints
is an extremely reprehensible thing. Let us not forget the
history of the Jukes family. Among the descendants of two
habitual criminals of the State of New York, there were 339
prostitutes, 181 chronic drunkards, 170 tramps, 118 criminals
and 86 brothel-keepers. Goddard observes that, in a certain
number of families where the father and mother were feeble-
minded, 470 children were mental defectives and only 6
normal. It is a definite crime to engender a long line of
physical and mental degenerates, gangsters or idiots. Dysgenism constitutes a capital offense. Addiction to opium,
morphia, cocaine or hashish is equivalent to suicide.

3 | *Laws of Life and Christian Morality.—Original Taints.
—Inevitable Suffering.*

There is a striking resemblance between the concept of sin
inspired by knowledge of the laws of our nature and the
Christian concept, although they spring from quite different
origins. One is the product of a purely rational and intellec-

tual operation; the other is based on intuition, inspiration and divine revelation. Yet the results of such different mental processes are, in some ways, almost identical. Both codes of conduct which derive from them ordain the same virtues and proscribe the same vices.

The morality of the Gospel is far from being a visionary's dream. Neither is it simply a pious practice which anyone is free to observe or to ignore. Its function is not, as Voltaire thought, to prevent the poor from killing the rich and to allow the latter to sleep peacefully in their beds. On the contrary, it represents a profound necessity of our being. It is, in fact, like those rules of conduct deduced from the fundamental laws of human nature, the indispensable condition for the survival of the individual and his descendants and for his spiritual development.

Nevertheless, it cannot, by itself alone, assure this survival. Religious faith cannot be the only guide of human conduct in the natural order. It has not succeeded in forming men and women capable of completely fulfilling their functions. We must render to God the things which are God's and to Caesar the things which are Caesar's. Science is as necessary as religion and reason as necessary as feeling. Biological morality is, in fact, more severe than the decalogue. Only by putting into practice the rules of conduct imposed by the laws of life are the evangelical virtues rendered possible.

Christian morality has, indeed, never claimed the exclusive guidance of men in the natural order. The success of life does not depend only on moral factors.

Yet even perfect submission to the rules imposed by the structure of our own bodies and minds, as well as to those of Christian morality, will not save us from suffering. The plan of the universe is not what human intelligence desires it to be; to behave ourselves rationally will not protect us from misfortune. Each individual contains in himself the whole past of the race; he has the defects as well as the qualities of his ancestors. He is born more or less burdened with hereditary taints. He suffers from an original sin whose weight he will carry all his life. This sin does not weigh equally heavily on all. Among the children of the same parents, it sometimes crushes one while remaining hardly perceptible in the others. The defects of some far-off ancestor may suddenly reappear after several generations and bring suffering to the innocent.

Not only do we suffer from hereditary defects but each one of us is exposed to the inevitable risks of his environment. These risks range from vicissitudes of climate to the jealousy and wickedness of his neighbors. Calamities fall alike on the just and the unjust but they show a certain preference for the ignorant, the lazy, the intemperate and the feeble. The will to behave according to the laws of life does not always insure that we shall be happy, for our knowledge of the order of the world is still rudimentary.

Human suffering could be greatly diminished by the intelligent application of science: in particular by eugenism and psychophysiology. Science is capable of giving man certain aids which dispose him to do good and avoid evil. It is imperative that society should make a systematic effort to alter those customs and institutions which violate the laws of life. Of course we shall never be able to suppress sorrows, worries, certain hereditary disease, old age and death. The good and the bad, criminals and saints alike, are exposed to the calamities inherent in the human condition. But these calamities wear a different face according to whether they knock at the door of the just, or that of the idle, the proud or the perverse. Before the just, their aspect loses its terror. He who completely fulfills the vocation of man, who obeys all the laws of life and particularly the law of spiritual development, often receives nervous resistance and mental balance as a reward. Sometimes he receives an ineffable peace, that peace which life gives to her elect as God gives His grace. Against that peace, misfortune can never prevail; in tribulations, in inevitable suffering and even in the anguish of dying it accompanies and sustains those who have been unflinchingly faithful to the silent behests of life.

4 | *Meaning of Virtue.*

Virtue is a very ancient datum of observation. Of course one still encounters virtue in modern society but there is very little place for it in communities which live under the banner of materialism. A society which puts economics first is not addicted to virtue, for virtue consists essentially in obedience to the laws of life. When man is reduced to economic activity, he no longer fully obeys those natural laws. Far from being a Utopian dream, virtue roots us firmly in reality. A virtuous individual is like an engine in good working order. It is to lack of virtue that the weakness and disorders of modern society are due.

There are as many virtues as there are human activities. All are essential just as all our physical and mental functions are essential. They have no natural hierarchy although they have been arbitrarily divided into groups. Plato recognized four principal virtues: prudence, justice, fortitude and temperance. These virtues were adopted by St. Ambrose and incorporated into Christian theology where they became the cardinal virtues. The Church added to them the three theological virtues of faith, hope and charity.

It is strange that the practice of virtue should not be taught in our schools since it is equally necessary to social and individual life.

Our material and spiritual needs vary. In certain countries and in certain circumstances, one virtue can momentarily become more important than another. Wherever the spirit of division and mutual hatred is rife, the most necessary virtues are courtesy, patience, forgiveness of injuries and brotherly love. In such regions as Normandy and Brittany, where alcoholism is bringing about the degeneration of a once notably vigorous people, the virtue of fortitude, which alone makes temperance possible, needs to be taught. All civilized peoples today badly need to practice prudence and eugenics. Plato considered prudence, along with justice, as the principle of all the other virtues. Its function is to harmonize the activities of mind and body and to restrain both from developing at each other's expense. Only the practice of this virtue can stop the breakup of Western civilization. In the time of Pericles, the Greeks practiced eugenics quite naturally and unconsciously; today eugenics should rank high among our preoccupations. Hygiene and medicine have lacked prudence by encouraging the breeding of the weak, the diseased and the degenerate with the result that the number of degenerates is constantly increasing. Eugenism has thus become indispensable to the welfare of the white races.

Thanks to the Puritans, virtue has acquired a bad reputation. It is confused with hypocrisy, intolerance, harshness and prudery. In actual fact, it is virilty, beauty and life. It protects individuals and social life, just as instinct protects wild animals, and is the very condition of our survival. It is as foolish not to be virtuous as to put water instead of oil into an internal combustion engine.

Ever since the morality of pleasure was substituted for pagan Stoicism and Christian morals, civilized people no longer perceive that virtue is a necessity. They think, like Rumen, that we have no obligation to be virtuous. The choice between virtue and vice should depend on each per-

son's self-interest and pleasure. Today we realize that virtue
is indeed obligatory for man exposes not only himself but his
country and his descendants to decadence and destruction
if he rebels against life's fundamental laws.

We are not isolated individuals; both in our families and
in society we are members one of another. Any single person who lowers himself by vice harms the entire group.
Similarly, the raising of any single life by virtue profits the
whole community. Tolerance of evil is a dangerous error
for no one is free to behave just as he pleases. Anyone who
allows himself to indulge in intemperance, idleness, slander
or any other vice should be considered as a public enemy.

Even the most corrupt societies still keep a definite sense
of the value of virtue. Heroes and martyrs are instinctively
honored by the crowd. Modern states have degenerated because, by drying up the springs of virtue in themselves, they
have refused to obey life.

CHAPTER FIVE

The Rules of Conduct

1	*Rules of Conduct Derive from the Triple Law of Life. —Character of These Rules.—Self-Discipline and Liberty.*

The rules of human conduct derive from the basic laws and constitute a guide for the perilous journey on which we are all engaged. To accomplish our destiny, it is not enough merely to guard prudently against road accidents. We must also cover before nightfall the distance assigned to each one of us. We must not only preserve life but propagate it; we must also increase and strengthen our spiritual forces.

There are no watertight compartments in our inmost nature. Nevertheless, we divide the rules of conduct into three groups: the discipline of our personal life, the precepts for human relations and the discipline of the transmission of life. Of course these are arbitrary divisions: the discipline of personal life, that is the inner life of the organs, the blood and the soul, merges with that of our relation with our parents and neighbors and with the requirements of the propagation of the race. Honesty, truth, love and unselfishness, which condition the highest communal existence, are the expression of a strong and harmonious personality. It is

102

the same with the physical and mental qualities which give an individual the power to hand on life in all its fullness.

Every rule of conduct has two aspects. It opposes certain tendencies and favors certain others. We ought to refuse to follow those ideas, desires and appetites which carry us in the opposite direction to the current of life. We should, by voluntary effort, avoid those faults and actions which are harmful to the conservation of our own life and that of others; to spiritual development and to the propagation of the race. The inhibition of bad tendencies and the correction of functional disorders are not, however, sufficient. We must also increase the quality, quantity and intensity of our lives. People become rich, not by saving, but by working and by making the money they have earned work instead of lying idle. Not to hate one's neighbor is good, but to love him is far better. The best way not to grow weaker is to increase one's strength. The rules of conduct must not only tell us what not to do, but also, and still more imperatively, what to do.

Like a child lost in a forest, modern man wanders at random in the world he has created. There are no signposts on our road to warn us of forbidden zones. Anyone, without realizing it, may cross that frontier which the very structure of life ordains for our thoughts as well as our deeds. To protect ourselves against this danger, a strict discipline is essential. There is no other way of avoiding the bogs, the quicksands and the precipices. We need a map and a guide for the dangerous journey of life.

What does the principle of the conservation of life demand of us?

First of all it demands that we respect life itself. It is forbidden to man to destroy himself or others. "Thou shalt not kill" is one of the Ten Commandments. There are many ways of killing. Civilization has presented us with more subtle methods of murder than those of our barbaric ancestors and those of the gangsters who flourish today in our towns. The profiteer who sends up the price of necessities, the financier who cheats poor people of their savings, the industrialist who does not protect his workmen against poisonous substances, the woman who has an abortion and the doctor who performs it are all murderers. Murderers, too, are the makers of harmful liquor and the wine growers who conspire with politicians to increase the consumption of drink; the sellers of dangerous drugs; the man who encourages his friend to drink; the employer who forces his workers to work and live in conditions disastrous to their bodies and minds.

It is forbidden not only to destroy life but to hinder it, to stifle it, to make it wretched and to impair its quality. This precept is infringed daily by parents whose egoism, ignorance and laziness deprive their children of moral and physiological education; by husbands who ill-treat or abandon their wives or who exhaust them by too frequent pregnancies; by wives whose bad temper, slovenliness and disorderliness make their husbands' daily life intolerable. It is also infringed by pedagogues who overload the young with a sterile and wearisome curriculum; by children who torture their parents by their ingratitude and spitefulness. All these acts are embryonic forms of murder. There are many other ways of doing violence to people's lives. Incessant mockery and backbiting, sly slandering, hate, contempt—all these deeply wound their victims, destroy their peace of mind and often permanently lessen the value of life for them. Though modern society underestimates the gravity of such offenses they are just as odious as stabbing one's brother in the back. The principle of preserving life discountenances suicide as much as murder. It condemns not only the brutal destruction of the self by the self, but all those thoughts, acts and habits which tend to lower our vitality, to disturb the balance of our nervous systems or our minds, to cause disease or to diminish the quality and the length of our lives. Pride and anger, for example, are harmful because they derange mental and nervous balance and falsify judgment. Egoism, avarice and envy contract the personality, obscure the moral sense and dwarf the intelligence. Sloth prevents the development of our inherited powers and brings ignorance, disorder and misery in its train. It is, together with intemperance, the principal enemy of modern man. Both are a form of protracted suicide. It is to these vices that the great nations partly owe their decline. In the years before the war they were the greatest consumers of alcoholic drink in the world. Alcoholism, nicotine poisoning, sexual excesses, the drug habit, mental dissipation and low morals all constitute extremely dangerous breaches of the law of self-preservation. These vices weaken the individual and mark him with a special stamp. The young Frenchman of the defeat: rude, slovenly, unshaven, slouching about with his hands in his pockets and a cigarette in the corner of his mouth, was all too representative of the anemic barbarism on which the France of those years prided herself. She had destroyed her own ability and strength. Her fate was inevitable, for she had committed the unforgivable sin. Nature annihilates those who abandon themselves. Suicide often takes a subtle and pleasent form such as abundance of food, soft living, complete economic security and absence of responsibilty. No one realized the dangers of the comfort we enjoyed in the years before the world war. Neither did they realize the dangers of the excessive eating and drinking to which everyone was addicted from infancy to old age. To have a safe position, exempt from responsibility, in some government department seemed to most people highly desirable. Yet this sort of existence is as dangerous as the drug habit both for the individual and the nation. There are also habits, apparently almost innocuous, which nevertheless diminish vital power. Such negative attitudes of mind as self-pity, jealousy, the habit of criticizing everyone and everything, unconstructive pessimism, react on the sympathetic nervous system and the endocrine glands. They can thus originate functional and even organic disorders. In the Middle Ages the Church considered *acedia* (or apathy) as sinful. On the same grounds as it forbids suicide, the principle of conserving life forbids any thoughts and moral attitudes which weaken our organs and our nervous systems.

3 | *Rules for the Conservation of Life.—Increase of Life in Oneself and Others.*

To preserve life, it is not enough to refrain from destroying it. We must also make it wider, deeper, bolder and more joyful. Strength is the only thing which allows man to rise higher. In the eyes of nature, it is the supreme virtue while weakness is the worst vice. The weak are destined to perish, for life loves only the strong. The strength we need does not resemble the muscular strength of the athlete, the moral strength of the ascetic or the intellectual strength of the philosopher and the scientist. It comprises stamina, harmony and suppleness of muscles, organs and mind along with the capacity to bear fatigue, hunger, sorrow and anxiety. It is the will to hope and to act, the solidarity of the body and soul which does not admit the possibility of defeat, the joy which permeates our whole being. How can we acquire this strength? The only way is by patient, dogged, daily effort; unconscious effort on the part of the heart, the glands and all the anatomical system; conscious effort on the part of the will, the intelligence and the muscles. One must learn little by little, by exercises repeated every day, to establish order in one's life, to accept one's self-imposed discipline and to be one's own master. One must also train oneself, by small and frequent efforts, to dominate one's feelings; one's nervousness, laziness, weariness and suffering. Such an apprenticeship is indispensable to any civilized person; the basic error of modern teaching is to have neglected it.

The rules to follow are many, but simple. They consist in leading our daily life as the structure of our body and mind demands. We must learn to endure heat, cold and fatigue; to walk, run and climb in all extremes of weather. We must also avoid as much as possible the artificial atmosphere of offices, flats and motorcars. In the choice of the quantity of food we eat we ought to follow modern principles of nutrition. We should sleep neither too much nor too little and in a quiet atmosphere. We should specialize in the work to which we are physically and mentally capable of adapting ourselves and do it as best we can. We should rest and amuse ourselves in such a way that rest and amusement do not become an additional fatigue or a total waste of time. We should avoid the exhibitionism of official sports but we should practice every day such exercises as those recommended by Hébert, which simultaneously develop organs, bones and muscles. We should also accomplish daily, outside of our professional work, some definite task of an intellectual, esthetic, moral or religious nature. Those who have the courage to order their existence thus will be magnificently rewarded. Life will give herself to them, as she gave herself to the inhabitants of ancient Greece, in her full strength and beauty.

The history of animals and men shows that the weak have no rights, not even the right to live on the land of their forefathers. The inhabitants of Normandy, Brittany and Anjou, the fairest, richest and most enviable provinces in France, have allowed life to grow feeble in themselves and in their children. If they do not become regenerate, history will once more repeat itself. Sooner or later they will be replaced by biologically stronger races. This will come about all the more easily because modern methods permit the swift deportation of whole populations far from their homes to regions which a rigorous climate and poor soil have emptied of their inhabitants.

Nature has no pity for alcoholics or for those who are lazy or feeble-minded. She favors those who are sober, alert, intelligent and enthusiastic; most of all, those who have the courage to take risks and who possess the will to succeed. She smiles on those who are ready to live hard and dangerously. Whoever refuses to take risks pays the penalty of loss of life in one form or another.

4 | *Rules for the Propagation of the Race.—Conception and Development of the Child.—Eugenism.*

The rules for the propagation of the race are as complex as the processes of generation and development. They are based on the peculiar characteristics of reproduction in the human species and on the needs of the young during their time of growth. They can be divided into three groups. The first deals with conception, the second with the birth of the child and its formation, the third with the environment indispensable to the material and spiritual life of the family.

The greater part of the hard task of carrying on the race falls on the woman. Yet she cannot abstain from this task without failing to fulfill the mission which is properly hers. That mission has been designated for probably more than a million years in her genital organs, her glands, her nervous system and in her whole mentality. To renounce motherhood is, for a woman, the gravest of errors. The outstanding sin of modern society has been to divert young girls from their proper function by giving them the same sort of physical, moral and intellectual education as boys. By doing so, it has implanted in them habits of life and thought which alienate them from their natural role.

To have a lucrative or brilliant career; to become an artist, doctor, lawyer, airwoman or schoolmistress is not a valid reason for violating the laws of propagation by means of contraceptive techniques. The more highly gifted the woman, physically and mentally, the more important it is that she should have several children. Furthermore, it is only through motherhood that she can attain her full organic and mental development. Motherhood is the only role in which she excels; in medicine, teaching, science, philosophy, aviation or business, she is nearly always man's inferior.

It is highly necessary that public opinion should not be indulgent toward couples who have too few children or none at all. It is still more important that women themselves should be conscious of their true role in society. We know, from the example of Italy, that neither taxes on bachelors and childless couples, nor economic and financial advantages given to large families, nor the protection of mothers and children, nor severe penalties for abortion and for birth-control propaganda stop the decline of the birth rate. Modern nations can only halt on the road to extinction through an awakening of conscience and understanding on the part of women themselves. The fate of the democracies lies in the hands of the girls of today.

How many children does the law of reproduction prescribe for each woman? Every woman should leave at least one daughter behind her to take her place. As all women are not fertile, and as many have a defective heredity, normal couples should have four or five children. The State should, for its own sake, give such couples very substantial financial help. To the others it should give none at all. We must guard ourselves from increasing the number of consumptives, alcoholics, idiots and degenerates who will become a heavier and heavier burden on the community by thoughtlessly distributed family allowances.

A declining birth rate is a degenerative disease which has affected all civilizations. It caused the downfall of ancient Greece and of the Roman Empire. At the present time it is devastating modern nations. The English population, for example, will be reduced by half in ninety years' time if the birth rate and death rate do not vary during this period. The disease is not, however, necessarily incurable since it is due to economic and social conditions, to contraceptive practices and to abortion. Consequently, its cure depends on the will of the State and above all on the will of women. The saving of our civilization demands the procreation, not only of sufficient children, but also of children of good caliber. Husbands and wives should choose life companions of such a type that their children will have a good heredity. Wild animals can mate purely at the bidding of their sexual appetites without any danger of dysgenism for, thanks to natural selection, the diseased and defective do not survive. This is not the case with domesticated animals and men. Both are carriers of hidden or visible hereditary taints.

Neither mutual sexual attraction nor even love are, by themselves, sufficient reason for justifying marriage. It is essential that, besides sexual attraction or love, there should be good heredity. A certain eugenism is imposed on modern peoples. The protection given to the diseased and the defective; the development of hygiene, of sanatoria and hospitals; the general comfort and the ease of modern life have allowed many tainted individuals, whose existence is undesirable for the future of the race, to reproduce themselves. It will be necessary to add the light of commonsense to public charity and medical zeal.

The law of propagation commands some people to have several children and others to have none at all. In the case of individuals with bad pedigrees, marriage between first cousins or between uncle and niece constitute, like incest, extremely grave faults. On the contrary, these faults would become virtues in human groups which were absolutely free of hereditary taints. Adultery is reprehensible both because it breaks up the social group vitally necessary to the well-being of the children and because it risks the introduction of inferior blood into a good stock. It would be a wise measure on the part of the government to encourage the establishment of the pedigree of every child and to take account of this pedigree in distributing family allowances. The government should also ensure that young people have sufficient knowledge of the laws of heredity. Each one should know that to marry into a family afflicted with madness, mental deficiency, tuberculosis or alcoholism is a major transgression against the law of propagation and that this transgression involves the guilty in an endless series of sorrows and calamities.

The excellence of one's ancestors is not, however, sufficient to ensure that one's children will be of good caliber. The future parents themselves must not be syphilitics, drunkards or drug-fiends. The drunkenness of wife or husband at the moment of fecundation is a positive crime, for children conceived in such conditions often suffer from incurable nervous or mental taints. Generally speaking, parents who are rash enough to ignore the obligations of eugenism are automatically punished by their own children.

5 | *Rules for the Propagation of the Species.—Birth and Formation of the Child.—The Family.*

The special physiological and psychological features of pregnancy and of the birth and growth of the child are what give the family its particular character. It is these too which impose clear-cut and unvarying rules of conduct on the members of this elementary social group. Father, mother and children constitute a kind of organism, an association of different but complementary entities. Like the organs of our body, they work for one another. But they only form a harmonious whole if, by voluntary effort, they fight against their natural selfishness, vanity, coarseness, intemperance, and nervous irritability. Unlike the bitch or the cow, a woman needs the help of her consort to provide for her during the final period of her pregnancy until after lactation.

A woman's period of fertility varies from thirty to forty years. During the first year of its life, a child is extremely frail. Subsequently it still needs constant care, attentive protection, gaiety and peace. Psychological shocks are extremely harmful to it. It develops very slowly; its formative period lasts at least eighteen years. Thus the task of reproducing the race demands the greater part of a woman's life. The ultimate reason for the permanence of marriage is this slow development of the young. To consider marriage as a temporary association which the parties can break at will is an error springing from ignorance of the way a child develops and of a mother's true function. Parents who upset their children's lives by their quarrels, their intemperateness, their adulteries, divorces and remarriages, seriously transgress the law of the propagation of life. The family organism is a collective individual of a very special character which should have a legal status in accordance with its structure and its function. One of the strangest aberrations of the French Revolution was to have made marriage a contract which could be dissolved like others, by its law of the 20th September 1792.

To develop in the best possible way, children need a stable and ordered family background. This order and stability can only be obtained by observing certain rules. First, by a prudent choice of partner; next, by getting rid of the egoism which makes married life impossible; lastly, by putting oneself in the material conditions necessary for the happy birth and bringing up of children. In modern society, employment of women, cramped housing, insecurity and the ignorance of parents make these conditions difficult to obtain. Thus the State should give generous aid to couples who are capable of having healthy and intelligent children. It is necessary, too, that future parents should realize the extent of their own ignorance and learn their difficult task of training the young. The bankruptcy of modern education is one reason for the disfavor into which the family has fallen.

Modern children constitute a truly insupportable burden for the family group. Their hardness, rudeness and ingratitude to their parents are the inevitable consequence of the parents' own selfishness, ignorance and weakness. The law of propagation demands of all young people who intend to marry a thorough moral and intellectual reform. This reform will be difficult and laborious but it is indispensable to their own well-being and to the survival of our civilization.

6 | *Rules for the Propagation of Life.—The Social Milieu.*

The maintenance of children and their physical and mental formation depend both on the family and on the milieu which surrounds it. The constituting of this milieu is society's most important task. The success of any society demands above all the cooperation and unity of its members. The conduct of each one of us should be ordered to the end of realizing this cooperation and unity.

Antisocial vices have spread in France in the most baleful way. They raise barriers between individuals and make it impossible for the community to survive. Envy and pride have caused just as disastrous divisions between peasants, workers and artisans as between generals, politicians, professors and scientists. Jealousy is responsible for the barrenness of our institutions because, by preventing the rise of the best men, it has put a premium on mediocrity. It is due to jealousy that, in all domains, men who were capable of becoming leaders and of organizing their nation have been eliminated. The inhabitants of one village, one town, one province, one state are jointly responsible for each other. Nevertheless, as a principle of conduct, joint responsibility has completely failed.

Nothing is more urgent than to put an end to this division. For a society to be prosperous, its members must be united to one another like the stones of a wall. But what cement will join men together in such a manner? The only cement firm enough is love, the love one sometimes finds existing between the members of one family but not extending to strangers. To love someone, said Aristotle, is to wish him well. It is strange that up to now humanity has refused to understand that to wish well to others is indispensable to the success of collective existence. Yet it knows that love of our neighbor and even of our enemy, forgiveness and charity are the essential basis of moral life. It is nearly two thousand years since it first learned these things. Those rare individuals who obey the Gospel commandment sometimes attract the respect of others, but in general they are considered fools or visionaries. No one realizes that this law of love constitutes the essential principle of the prosperity of human groups and the very condition of their survival.

Why then is a precept so undoubtedly true not applied? Probably it has remained inapplicable because we have never tried to make it possible to apply it. The precept of loving one's neighbor has a double aspect. Explicitly, it commands everyone to love others but, implicitly, it also commands everyone to make themselves worthy of being loved. It is beyond human powers to love the average product of industrial civilization; that is to say, an individual who is selfish, coarse, proud, lazy, envious, intemperate, ill-natured and lubricous. Mutual love will remain a Utopian ideal until we make an effort to give up the habits which render us odious to other people. It is not by elaborating new ideologies or by reforming our political institutions that we shall build a better society. What we must do is to reform our own selves and free ourselves from those vices which separate us from one another. Then it will be possible for neighbor to love neighbor; for workmen to love their employers and employers to love their workmen. Love alone is capable of installing in human societies the order which instinct has established for millions of years among the communities of ants and bees.

	Rules for Development of Spirit in the Individual.—
7	Physical, Physiological and Mental Obstacles.—How Find One's Soul?—Self-Discipline.—Development of Feeling.—Development of Intellect.—Hero-Worship. —Intuition.—Search for Beauty and for God.

Though the development of the spirit is as strict an obligation as the other two, it is one of which we take very little account. Schools and universities are content to cultivate the intellect but the intellect is not equivalent to the spirit which in every way transcends it. It is the nonlogical activities of the mind which constitute the real substratum of the personality. The first commandment of the law of spiritual development is that everyone should realize the full measure of his inherited mental capacities, be these great or small. This obligation is universal. It applies equally to young and old, rich and poor, ignorant and learned. This voluntary raising of our spiritual level is our only way of helping to save Western civilization and of saving descendants from even greater calamities than those we are suffering ourselves.

The first thing we must do is to remove the obstacles which hinder our spiritual development. Some of these obstacles are chemical or physiological; others are mental. Nervous and mental equilibrium are closely related. Both depend simultaneously on the tissues, the blood, the intellect and the feelings. We must impose calmness on our bodies just as much as on our thoughts. It is a great mistake to let children become agitated or nervous. Organic and mental functions react reciprocally. The harmony of the organic function is indispensable to mental serenity. Thus all habits which may cause deterioration in the tissues and the body fluids must be avoided. In particular we must avoid excessive indulgence in alcohol, tobacco and food, indeed in any overindulgence which may ultimately cause the various forms of sclerosis and bring on premature old age.

Secondly, it is equally necessary to renounce those mental attitudes which so atrophy the consciousness that they amount to spiritual suicide. Laziness is particularly lethal. Laziness does not only consist in doing nothing, in sleeping too long, in working badly or not at all, but also in devoting our leisure to stupid and useless things. Endless chattering, card-playing, dancing, rushing about aimlessly in motorcars, abusing the movies and the radio—all these reduce the intelligence. It is also dangerous to have a smattering of too many subjects without acquiring a real knowledge of any one. We need to defend ourselves against the temptations provided by the rapidity of communication, by the number of magazines and newspapers, by the motorcar, the airplane and the telephone, to multiply to excess the number of ideas, feelings, things and people which enter into our daily lives. Carried beyond certain limits, specialization can be just as much an obstacle to spiritual development as too wide a field of interests. Today, of course, we are all to some extent specialists. We are not obliged to confine ourselves entirely to our own subject; nothing prevents us from devoting our leisure to cultivating the intellectual, moral, esthetic and religious activities which form the substratum of personality.

Of all bad habits, the most harmful to spiritual progress are those of lying, intriguing, slandering and betraying one's neighbors and of turning everything to one's own immediate advantage. The spirit can never develop in an atmosphere of corruption and falsehood.

How then can we escape the deleterious influence of the modern world? By observing a rule similar to the one which the Stoic philosophers and the early Christians imposed on themselves; by uniting oneself with those who have the same ideals and by submitting to a strict discipline. For example, by not listening to the lies of the radio, by reading in the paper only the news which is useful to know, by reading books and articles only by writers known for their competence and honesty, by acquiring some knowledge of modern techniques of propaganda so as to be proof against them —in fact, by being resolutely nonconformist. It is impossible to accept the modes of life and thought which have been disseminated from the cities into the very depths of the country without being spiritually annihilated. In order to set out on the upward road, we must first give up the habits and vices which inhibit the free movement of the spirit.

These obstacles once removed, we must begin the ascent ordained by the fundamental tendencies of life. A human being has the strange privilege of being able to fashion his body and soul, if he so wishes, by the help of his soul itself. One can learn to manage oneself as one learns to manage an airplane. But only those who already possess self-mastery can profitably venture on this apprenticeship. To make one's spirit grow, there is no need to be learned or to possess a great intellect; all that is needed is the will. All of us, at certain moments of our lives, need to take advice and to receive help from other people. But no one but ourselves can develop and discipline the intellectual and affective activities which are the essence of personality.

In this highly delicate enterprise, we must first discover our own soul. Everyone can make this contact, no matter what his sorrows or weariness, no matter how imposing or modest his occupation. All that is needed is, for a few minutes morning and night, to silence the noises of the world, to retire into oneself, to recognize one's errors and to make one's plan of action. This is the time when those who know how to pray should do so. "No man has ever prayed without learning something," said Emerson. Prayer always has an effect even if it is not the effect we desire. This is why we ought to accustom children very early in their lives to short periods of silence and recollection and, above all, of prayer. Undoubtedly, it is difficult to find the path which leads down into our innermost soul. But once initiated, any man, whenever he wishes, can penetrate to the peaceful land which extends beyond the images of things and the babble of words. Then, little by little, the darkness thins, and, like a quiet stream, light begins to flow in the midst of silence. The first step, then, is not to cultivate one's intelligence but to construct in oneself the affective framework which will serve as a support for all the other elements of the spirit. The moral sense is as necessary as sight or hearing. One must accustom oneself to distinguish as clearly between right and wrong as between light and darkness. Then one must impose upon oneself the duty of avoiding evil and doing good.

Avoiding evil demands a good organic and mental constitution. The finest development of body and mind is only possible with the help of asceticism. Athletes, men of science, monks, all submit themselves to strict rules of life and thought. No excess is permitted to those who desire to rise to spiritual heights. Self-discipline is always rewarded by a strength which brings an inexpressible, silent inner joy which becomes the dominant tone of life. However strange such a physiological and mental attitude may seem to modern pedagogues and sociologists, it is none the less the essential foundation of a full personality. It is like an airdrome from which the spirit can take flight.

Little by little, the qualities which give the character its greatness must be made to grow. The Church, with her twenty centuries of experience, rightly places self-examination, purification of mind and feelings and the will to make moral progress at the beginning of the upward path. It is essential to obey this precept and then to proceed to acquiring intellectual integrity, love of truth and loyalty.

Even more than philosophers and priests, scientists engaged in experimental research know how indispensable these qualities are. A single sin, however venial, against truth is promptly punished by the failure of the experiment. In the dangers of our communal, as of our individual life, truth alone can save us.

Slowly the road winds upward through the years. At the outset, many are sucked down into bogs, fall over precipices or lie down in the soft grass and go to sleep for ever. In joy or sorrow, health or sickness, prosperity or the reverse, the effort must still continue. One must rise after every fall and gradually acquire courage, faith, the will to succeed and the capacity to love. Last of all, one must acquire detachment. These nonrational elements of the spirit constitute the magnetism of the personality. Logic never attracts men to the point of carrying them away. Neither Kant, Bergson nor Pasteur were loved by their disciples as Napoleon was loved by his soldiers. Only by their capacity for love, justice and detachment can the humble become superior to the great and powerful and the powerful themselves become great.

The development of the intelligence is quite as imperative as that of the feelings. While we are forging our character we should also be developing our mental activities, activities which school has probably atrophied almost as much as our moral ones. It is only when the individual has escaped from the hands of the professors and is free of examinations and lectures that he can begin his intellectual education. He has to begin by training himself to see, feel, listen, observe and judge; in other words, to make contact with reality.

Manual work is indispensable to everyone, for precision of gesture assists precision of thought. But no one, once he has mastered the technique of any craft, should limit himself only to that technique. A sculptor can, like Michelangelo, also be a painter and an architect. Nothing prevents a financier from following the example of Lavoisier and becoming a chemist or a physicist. The time we waste in idle talk, in illusory worldly duties, in the movies or on the golf course would allow us, if we used it properly, to know the world in which we live and the one in which our forefathers lived. Instead of reading papers and magazines written to please the mentally atrophied, we could learn, from technical books and journals or from reputable works of popular science, things which deal with our own and our children's lives and with the world about us. Then we should have the joy of seeing our horizon extend in the most wonderful way. We should know how the universe of which we form part is constituted and how we are constituted ourselves. We should learn how to develop the hidden powers of our bodies and our souls, how to make our children finer beings than ourselves. No one whose material conditions permit him to widen his scope of knowledge has the right to remain an ignorant barbarian. School certificates and degrees are not the only things which have the power to deliver us from this unenlightened state.

Periods of decadence are characterized by the mediocrity of their leading men. The mass suffers if it has no one to admire them, for hero-worship is a natural human need and also an essential condition of mental progress. In the democratic countries there is no man capable of serving as a model to the young. Happily, society comprises not only the living but the dead, and the great dead still live in our midst. We can contemplate them and listen to them at will. Are they not present in the splendor of the Mont-Saint-Michel, in the luminous grandeur of the cathedral of Our Lady of Chartres, in the stern beauty of the Château de Tonquedec? Is it not better to keep company with Roland,

Charlemagne, Dante, Joan of Arc, Goethe and Pasteur than with the film stars? In the lives of scholars, heroes and saints, there is an inexhaustible reserve of spiritual energy. These men are like mountains which rise above the plain. They show how high we should try to climb and how noble is the goal toward which human consciousness naturally aspires. Only such men can give our interior life the spiritual food it needs.

The spirit contains elements less known and understood than intelligence, moral sense or character. These elements are quite impossible to express in words. They are intuitions, instinctive impulses, sometimes even extrasensorial perceptions of reality. The strength of the individual and of the nation comes from the richness of this substratum of the spirit. This indefinable spiritual energy is not found in nations who wish to express everything in clear-cut formulas. It has disappeared in France because the French obstinately refuse the irrational; they deny reality to anything which words are powerless to describe. Pascal was nearer to reality than Descartes: poets and mystics know more of man than the physiologists. Those who desire to rise as high as our human condition allows must renounce intellectual pride. They must dispel the illusion of the omnipotence of clear thinking and abjure their belief in the absolute power of logic. Lastly they must increase their own sense of the beautiful and the holy.

One cannot learn to love beauty or to love God as one learns arithmetic. The sense of beauty can only be given by beauty itself. Beauty is to be found everywhere. It is in the prairies of Canada as in the woods of the Ile-de-France; about the bay of San Francisco as on the shores of Corsica. Today, thanks to the advance of technology, even the ineffable ugliness of the factories of Chicago or of the Paris suburbs can shine with reflected beauty. Anyone can hear the works of Palestrina or Beethoven or any other classical masterpiece when he chooses. Without leaving one's arm-chair, one can travel in the most magnificent countries on earth. It costs hardly anything to buy the works of Virgil, Dante, Shakespeare or Goethe. Poor people who live in noisy industrial towns or in the most isolated country can, just as easily as the rich, develop their sense of beauty and penetrate those mental realms which transcend the intellect. We can all break the mold into which we were forced at school and let our souls escape into that world which was already familiar to our Cro-Magnon ancestors. The love of beauty leads its chosen further than the love of syllogisms for it sweeps our spirit toward heroism, renunciation and the absolute beauty which is God.

Only on the wings of mysticism can the spirit soar to its full height. This is where the role of religion becomes clearly defined. For this flight in the intellectual stratosphere beyond the four dimensions of space and time and beyond reason is dangerous. The techniques of religion, that is to say of the union of the soul with God, have been developed, step by step, over the course of thousands of years. No one can venture alone without grave risk in the obscure realm of the holy. Without an experienced guide there is serious risk of losing oneself in the marshes or of straying irrevocably into the road that leads to madness. In his sojourn in Paradise, Dante was led by Beatrice.

To sum up, the law of spiritual ascent lays on each one of us the duty of developing the whole range of his mental activities by the effort of his own will. It is a fundamental rule not to limit this effort to only one aspect of consciousness. Exclusive cultivation of either intellect or feeling is equally to be condemned. It is dangerous to be exclusively an intellectual or a mystic, a logician or an intuitive, a scientist or a poet. It is by the simultaneous upward trend of his intellectual, moral, esthetic and religious faculty that each one can attain the highest level compatible with his inherited latent powers.

8 | *Rules for the Development of Spirit in the Race.—We Must Not Arrest the Mental Progress of our Descendants.—Improvement of Environment.—How to Increase Spiritual Power.*

How can we contribute to the spiritual progress of our children and our children's children? Our first duty is to put no obstacle in the way of this progress. It is far from certain whether the development of the spirit in living forms is inevitable. We are totally ignorant of the nature of the factors which made the volume of the brain of certain mammals quadruple itself in some millions of years and which emancipated our ancestors from the automatism of animal instinct. Neither do we know under what influence man raised himself from the mental state of Pithecanthropus or Sinanthropus to that of Leonardo da Vinci, Pascal or Napoleon. Is it within man's power to arrest this evolution? How does the artificiality of modern life react on the anatomical and functional progress of the species? At the moment we can give no answer to these questions. It is wise, however, to ask ourselves whether the suppression of natural ways of life does not offer an insuperable obstacle to the evolutionary forces of spirit. Perhaps the spontaneous rise of consciousness in the race may come to an end through our own fault. What rule of conduct must we adopt to avoid this disaster?

At the moment we can only contribute to our mental progress by eugenics and by improving the environment. The knowledge and practice of eugenics are strictly obligatory. Eugenism is an indispensable virtue if we are to save Western civilization. It does not indeed raise the spiritual level of the élite but it increases the number of those who attain this level. There is no better way of promoting the greatness of a nation than by increasing the number of its more highly gifted citizens.

The second way of helping the mental strength of our descendants to accrue is to procure for everyone conditions of life which permit the highest development of his affective and intellectual possibilities. For a child to develop to its utmost, it needs a certain stability of life. The family must be rooted once more in the soil. Everyone should be able to have a house, however small, and make himself a garden. Everyone who already has a farm should beautify it. He should adorn it with flowers, pave the road which leads to it, destroy the briars which choke the hedges, break up the boulders which hinder the passage of the plow, and plant trees whose branches will shade his great-grandchildren. Finally, the works of art, the old houses, the splendid buildings and cathedrals in which the soul of our forefathers expressed itself must be piously preserved. We should also set ourselves against the profanation of the rivers, the tranquil hills and the forests which were the cradle of our ancestors. But our most sacred duty is to bring about a revolution in teaching which will make the school, instead of a dreary factory for certificates and diplomas, a center of moral, intellectual, esthetic and religious education.

Neither eugenics nor the improvement of the milieu will make the spirit rise higher than the level it shows in the most highly gifted among modern men. The progress of hygiene has not made us live longer but merely increased the average duration of life. To increase the intelligence of the race, we should have to find the secret of speeding up the natural march of evolution. Mind has not grown proportionately to the complexity of the problems to be solved. But such a growth is not impossible. We have two methods at our disposition to produce human beings mentally superior to all those who have hitherto existed on the earth. The first is the improvement of the individual; the second, that of the race.

Perhaps the moment has come for scientists to see whether it is possible to modify the quality of the brain matter and of the endocrine glands in such a way as to improve the mind. Perhaps one day we shall be able to make great men just as bees make queens. Of course such acquired qualities could not be hereditarily transmitted. As to the race, up to the present we know no means of making it progress artificially in the way it has progressed naturally in the course of evolution. All the mutations experimentally produced in animals have been regressive. We have, in fact, no knowledge whatsoever of the factors which have determined the rise of mind in the animal series. From now on, we ought to engage our greatest biologists in research on the secret factors of evolution; in other words, in the bold enterprise of increasing the strength and quality of mind in civilized man.

9 | *How to Adapt These Rules to Each Individual.— Interior Conflicts.—The Supreme Rule.—Spiritual Direction.*

Since each individual is different from all the rest, no code of conduct can be indiscriminately applied to all. Some have such highly individual temperaments that the customary rules cannot be applied to them without special adaptation. At first sight, it would seem that rules as universal as the three we have been discussing applied to all men of all races at all times. Nevertheless, this is not so. The history of Europe and America shows many examples of individuals who have transgressed these laws without bringing catastrophes either on themselves or on their neighbors. On the contrary, some of these transgressions have been immensely profitable both to society and to the race. St. Francis of Assisi did more for humanity by praying and begging than if he had been the father of a large family. It was also better that Amundsen should have sacrificed himself in the hope of saving Nobile than that he should have lived quietly at home to an advanced age. Though the laws of conservation and propagation are imperative, they nevertheless allow of exceptions. The law of spiritual development, on the contrary, is inflexible. Sometimes it is permissible to sacrifice life to the spirit but it is always forbidden to sacrifice the spirit to save one's life.

What course should we adopt when opposition arises in our innermost souls between the orders imposed by the basic laws of life? We must behave as the very structure of things demands of us. We know that there is a hierarchy in our natural duties. The life of an individual is less important than that of his descendants for nature in general sacrifices the individual to its progeny. When everyone prefers his own life to that of the nation, as happened in Rome, the nation collapses. In the human species, spiritual development is the supreme law. To convince oneself that this is so one only needs to observe the state of decline into which a population, infected at once with lack of moral discipline and intellectual infantilism, naturally falls.

The call of the spirit manifests itself more imperiously in many individuals than the call of life. Those who die to save a civilization respond magnificently to this call. So too do the legions of men and women who, in all ages, have transgressed the law of reproduction in order to pursue an ideal of patriotism, charity, beauty or love. Such is the soldier who dies weapon in hand; such are those who become poor and help the poor like Francis of Assisi or Vincent de Paul; such are those who, following the example of St. Benedict, dedicated themselves to God in the religious life.

What rule imposes itself today on those who prefer other duties to that of reproducing life; to those men, and particularly those women, who feel impelled to devote their life to science, charity or religion? As their number is relatively small in proportion to the whole population, it is permissible for them to obey the call of the spirit. We need apostles who will put themselves entirely at the service of children, mothers, the old and the abandoned. We also need brave and single-hearted enthusiasts capable of abandoning the world to devote themselves to the discovery and apprehension of reality, in laboratories, and monasteries. For the clever, the cunning and the prudent have made a resounding failure and our world is crumbling.

Sometimes subtler conflicts between the different mental activities arise: for example, between reason and feeling. What relative importance should be given to intellectual culture and to moral, esthetic and religious? Ought not certain of the nonintellectual activities of the spirit be developed in preference to others according to a person's temperament? Experience shows that the moral framework is more important both for the individual and for his social group than scientific, literary or philosophical knowledge.

Certainly the adapting of rules of conduct to each individual is not always an easy task. The laws of mental life are not as sharply defined as those of chemistry or physiology. A given rule has not the same relevance for a child, an adult or an old person. Nor can it be applied in just the same way to impulsive, scrupulous, depressed, bold or timid natures. The majority of human beings need a guide not only in their spiritual and social conduct but also in their physiological behavior. Very few are capable of directing themselves entirely on their own. Unfortunately, in modern society, there exist no men who specialize in being wise and in helping others with their wisdom. In bygone days, some old family doctors were sufficiently honest and had a wide enough knowledge of life to play the part of spiritual and temporal directors. But today the doctor has become a tradesman. No one would dream of asking a nose or liver or lung specialist for advice on the subject of his personal difficulties. As to the doctors who specialize in the whole behavior of the individual, such as the psychoanalysts, their intervention is sometimes useful, sometimes disastrous, and usually inadequate.

To teach men how to conduct their lives, we need guides who combine a knowledge of the modern world with the science of the doctor, the wisdom of the philosopher and the conscience of the priest; in other words, ascetics who have experience of life and are learned in the science of man. Perhaps a religious order whose members possessed a character at once scientific and sacerdotal should be founded for this very end. These men, when they had reached the threshold of old age, would be qualified to serve as guides to the vast flock of those who wander in universal confusion. It would be incumbent on such men to adjust the general rules of the conduct of life to the needs of each individual.

CHAPTER SIX

Putting the Rules of Conduct into Practice

	Difficulty of Rational Conduct.—Obstacles in Our-
1	*selves.—Obstacles We Meet in the World about Us.*

At the moment it is highly necessary that everyone should put the rules of conduct into practice in his daily life; that he should submit to a freely accepted, but strict discipline. Are we modern men capable of such an effort? Have we the intelligence and energy to give up the habits we find so pleasant and convenient? To behave rationally in the mental and material milieu created by modern society demands positive heroism. As I have written elsewhere, "Humanity has become master of its destiny. But will it be capable of using the immense forces of science to its own profit? To begin a new stage of growth, it is obliged to remake itself. And it cannot remake itself without suffering. It is at the same time the marble and the sculptor. To take on its true face, it must strike splinters out of its own substance with great blows of the chisel." Can we still make such an effort? Have we the intelligence and the strength to break the chain of the habits which bind us? We love freedom and ease; any constraint is painful to us. We have had neither the wisdom nor the courage to submit ourselves to laws. The

130

same thing has occurred at the end of all civilizations. When man frees himself from the necessities of primitive life by his intelligence and his inventions, he does not think of replacing the discipline imposed by nature. In ancient Greece and Rome, for example, the asceticism of the Stoics was only practiced by a negligible part of the population. The disciples of Zeno, Epictetus and Marcus Aurelius remained always very few. It is true that, in spite of its severity, Christian morality had a prodigious success; it gave Western civilization its particular structure. Though its influence was powerful, it did not resist the change in physical conditions and mental climate brought about by the progress of science and technology. As soon as rebellion becomes materially possible, man revolts against all discipline.

It is in our own selves that the greatest obstacles to the practicing of rules of conduct arise. It is extremely difficult for man to understand those things which, in his heart of hearts, he does not wish to understand. He instinctively closes his intelligence to the knowledge of any facts which would oblige him to give up anything he finds pleasurable. For example he refuses to admit that it is dangerous to gorge himself with wine or beer, to smoke incessantly, to lie, to slander his neighbor and to make himself odious to others by his selfishness and rudeness. One of the worst disorders of the spirit is to seek only those aspects we find agreeable both in ourselves and in the things about us. It is fatal to confuse the artificial needs created by our milieu with the fundamental needs of our nature; to pursue the immediate and illusory advantage instead of the distant and real one. We have no desire to see ourselves as we are; we are blinded by vanity and self-complacency. We can see no necessity to discipline ourselves and to change our way of behavior. Of course one cannot avoid work; one cannot earn money or acquire comfort without imposing certain rules on oneself.

But modern man finds it much easier to see the need for restraint when it is a question of satisfying his vanity or his passions than when it comes to acquiring health, intelligence or goodness. A man who willingly submits to the necessary training for winning a race may refuse to make any effort to train himself to be truthful or to fight his churlishness or his egoism. It almost seems as if our intelligence becomes paralyzed as soon as we apply it to ourselves.

Rational conduct is also hindered by the adverse forces of the environment in which we live. Our reawakening will have to come about in the very conditions which have brought about our decline. The moral climate of the community and the spirit of its institutions have not changed nor will they change until we have transformed them. Thus we must begin to practice the rules of conduct in an antagonistic milieu.

Society never fails to erect the barrier of its opposition against all nonconformists. In all ages, heretics have been burned. Today as hitherto, inventors die in want and prophets are stoned. The fact is that those who obey the laws of life will inevitably bring about the downfall of the present order. Naturally they are regarded as enemies by the great mass of the mediocre who live in ignorance, stupidity and corruption. Above all, they are considered as such by the wily who profit from this corruption, stupidity and ignorance.

At the present moment, we live in a world that is hostile to life. We exist in an environment ill-adapted to the real needs of our bodies and souls; among the crowd which wants above all to continue the regime of go-as-you-please, laziness and amoralism.

The enormous cataclysm of the world war has not recalled us to a sense of the real. Like a storm cloud, a strange madness darkens our intelligence. The absurd revolt of civilized people against the laws of life continues to spread. There is the same conflict between modern society and the rational conduct of life as there was between Roman society and Christian morality in the fourth century. Eating, drinking, chariot-racing and gladiatorial combats were the only pre-occupations of the Romans of the Decadence. Our own are identical and the civilization built up by science and technology is disintegrating like the civilizations of the past. Like the Romans, we do not realize the necessity to recreate ourselves. Would a return to more primitive conditions of life and to the hardships caused by cold and hunger remove some of the obstacles which prevent us from carrying out the rules of conduct?

2 | *How to Overcome These Obstacles.—Impotence of Reason.—The true Mainsprings of Our Actions.—The Power of Feeling.—The Pursuit of Self-Interest.*

Obedience to natural laws demands a discipline more exacting than that of the Stoics and quite as hard as that of the Christians during the first centuries of the Church. How shall we overcome our aversion to restraint, privations and suffering? Logic will not help us sufficiently. Men like Socrates who are capable of preferring reason to life are highly exceptional. No one completely immolates himself in the cause of scientific truth. Galileo himself refused to be martyred. The barriers raised by ignorance, cowardice and sloth are never overthrown by logic. When an idea succeeds in transforming men's conduct, it is because it contains elements which are affective as well as logical. Karl Marx was both a philosopher and a passionate revolutionary. Thus Communism has all the force of a religion.

It is faith and not reason which impels men to action. It is not the intelligence which will give us strength to live according to the order of things. Intelligence is content to point out the road but never drives us along it. In life, pure intellectuals behave like paralytics watching a race. They see the goal clearly but they are incapable of running on the track. Juggling with words is a sterile pastime. The love of abstractions engenders impotence.

We shall never conquer the difficulties which confront the nonconformist unless the impetus of feeling rises like a tide in the depths of our soul. The mainsprings of action belong to the affective order. In Plato himself they were not purely and simply rational. To act wisely, we need both feeling and reason for, without reason, sentiment can just as easily lead us to the bottom of the ocean as up into the stratosphere. We are driven to act by our elementary need; the need for food and water, for shelter, security, freedom and adventure. We are also driven by those simultaneous impulses of the spirit, the endocrine glands, the nervous system and the blood which we call jealousy, fear, hate or love. The need to know has impelled man in spite of himself along the road to inventions and discoveries. It was through this curiosity that we emerged from our primitive barbarism. The scientist is inspired neither by the love of humanity nor by the love of profit but by the need to ferret things out, to search and explore. Nevertheless, feeling becomes dangerous when not guided by reason. Jealousy, for example, can cause greater disasters than an epidemic of influenza. Everyone makes a greater effort to hurt other people than to help himself. Like hatred, jealousy is forbidden by the laws of life because it is essentially destructive. There are only two constructive passions; one is love, the other fear.

Only love has the power to throw down those ramparts behind which our egoism takes cover; to inflame our en-

thusiasm, to make us walk joyfully in the *via dolorosa* of
sacrifice. It is for love of its mother that a small child behaves well. The Christian submits to an arduous moral discipline for the love of God. But it is impossible to love an
abstraction. One will sacrifice oneself for one's family or
friends, for one's leader, for one's country or for God, but
not for an idea. The martyrs who died for Christ would not
have given their lives for the natural law. An abstraction
does not become a motivating force unless it contains a
religious element. This is why Christian morality is incomparably more powerful than lay morality. Thus man will
never enthusiastically obey the laws of rational conduct
unless he considers the laws of life as the commands of a
personal God. Unfortunately, most modern men are incapable of acting for the love of their neighbors, of their country
or of God for the only thing they love is themselves.

The love of oneself can also be a force. Its corollary is
fear and fear, like love, engenders action. Perhaps it will be
fear which will make civilized men rationalize their behavior. At certain moments, the only people who are not
afraid are madmen. No epoch of history has ever been so
terrifying. Never have greater cataclysms been unleashed.
For many years the knell has been tolling behind the threatening clouds on the horizon but we have deliberately shut
our ears. Whom the gods wish to destroy, they first make
mad. Then wars break out and the face of the world changes.
The hour of chaos is approaching. Nevertheless, we must try
at all costs to save ourselves and our children from the indescribable sufferings which accompany the agony of nations.
If we are to avoid these otherwise inevitable catastrophes,
we must recover our ancient strength. Perhaps fear will bring
us the necessary wisdom to recover it by submitting humbly
to the laws of life.

If it were intelligent, egoism might, like love or fear, induce us to behave more reasonably for nothing is more personally advantageous than to obey the natural law. Egoism is nothing more than an exaggeration or perversion of life's tendency to preserve itself. In its usual aspect it is a vice destructive to the community but in its less crude form it is a virtue. If we were completely lacking in egoism, we should be incapable of living. This natural egoism impels man to an untiring search for his material or spiritual profit; it is a necessary tendency which displays itself in the saint as well as the gangster. The pursuit of happiness is the pursuit of what is advantageous to health, freedom and beauty. And these goods are precisely those which we find through obedience to the laws of our nature. Unfortunately, the benefits of this obedience are not immediately obvious. They only manifest themselves slowly in the course of the life of the individual and the race. Generally speaking, egoism is not intelligent enough to distinguish the pleasurable from the useful, the real need from the artificial, the passing good from the permanent. It does not realize that rational behavior will bring us all the happiness compatible with our human state. As Socrates taught, duty is interwoven with pleasure and profit. It is to our own interest to observe the rules derived from natural laws. The moment has come when we must either accept decline and death or we must overthrow all the obstacles which oppose our revival.

3 | *Technique of Transforming Oneself.—Progress of the Adult.—Progress of the Child.—Oases of Rational Conduct.*

When the house is on fire, everyone leaves what he is doing to fight the flames. In the same way, when great social cataclysms are unleashed, we ought to suspend all other business and go into action. How can we save ourselves and those who belong to us? "For the first time in the history of the world a civilization which has arrived at the beginning of its decline can discern the causes of its decay. Perhaps it will know how to use this knowledge and avoid, thanks to the marvelous forces of science, the destiny common to all the great peoples of the past. We ought to set out immediately on a new path." [1] Before we can set out on this new path we must begin by transforming ourselves. It is impossible for us to free ourselves immediately from the errors of the past, and from the institutions which carry the indelible imprint of these errors for we are already weakened and deformed by habits contracted from our infancy. We are neither intelligent nor energetic enough to break the mold into which modern society has poured us. But we are, up to a point, masters of our actions. By an effort of will, everyone can change his habits of life and thought. It is only after such an inner renewal that we shall become capable of reforming our institutions. Revolutions do not begin in the tumult of the market place but in the inmost heart of a few men. Communism ripened slowly in the solitary meditations of Karl Marx and Engels. Thought only becomes creative if it overflows from the soul; inspiration needs the silence of the interior life. Modern man has declined because he has lacked this inspiration. To rebuild our civilization we must first rebuild ourselves according to the pattern laid down by life.

It is impossible to rationalize one's behavior without a proper technique. To acquire this technique is just as laborious as to acquire physical or mental culture.

We do not hesitate to devote several years to learning mathematics, history, experimental sciences or philosophy.

[1] *Man the Unknown.*

Equally we spend a great deal of time in learning the techniques of gymnastics, swimming, football, skiing or golf. Young people willingly accept university examinations or the tests necessary to obtain a driving license or a flying certificate. But they have not yet realized that the technique of conducting one's life is more difficult than any of these.

To learn how to be strong, intelligent and balanced; how to resist fatigue; how to avoid making oneself detestable to others, is no less essential than eating, sleeping, studying at school or working in office, farm or factory. The fight against egoism, for example, demands more skill than the fight against typhus or cholera. It is just as difficult to accustom oneself to a moderate use of wine, alcohol and tobacco as to pursue the study of higher mathematics.

The most effective way to live reasonably is every morning to make a plan of one's day and every night to examine the results obtained. Just as we know in advance what time our work begins and ends, what people we shall see, what we shall eat and drink and how much money we shall make, so we should also foresee certain other things. We should plan ahead what help we can give to others, how we can discourage the spite and malice in our midst; how we can fight our own selfishness and churlishness; what physical exercise we shall take and how we can curb our tendency to overindulgence.

Moral dirtiness is as repulsive as physical dirtiness. Before beginning a new day, each one of us should wash morally as well as physically.

Laying down a schedule is not enough; we must also observe how far we have carried out our program and how we have disobeyed the rules we have set ourselves. Some people make a point of doing physical exercises when they get up and before going to bed. It is no less important to devote some minutes every day to the progress of our moral, intellectual and psychological activities. This method has a powerful effect on the development of consciousness.

By meditating every day on the direction to be freely given to all one's actions and by forcing oneself to follow strictly the lines of conduct thus traced, one simultaneously strengthens the intelligence and the will. We begin to develop, in the depths of our soul, a secret domain where we come face to face with our naked self. Our success in carrying out the rules of behavior depends on the intensity of this interior life.

Just as the tradesman keeps his account books and the scientist his experimental notebook, so every single individual ought to register every day the good and evil for which he has been responsible. Above all he should record the amount of joy or sorrow, anxiety or peace, hate or love which he has given his family and his neighbors. It is by the patient application of these techniques that the transformation of our bodies and souls will gradually become a reality.

This transformation will never be complete. It is impossible for a grown-up person to efface all the traces of a faulty psychological, moral or intellectual formation. Moreover, bad habits cannot be entirely uprooted. The only people who are able to behave perfectly reasonably are those who have been accustomed from childhood to obey the laws of life. This is why our first preoccupation must be to transform education, to train our children far better than we have been trained ourselves.

In the first years of life this task falls exclusively on the parents. They cannot carry it out unless they themselves are initiated, and if they have not learned the techniques of the organic and mental formation of children, techniques which vary according to age, sex and environment. It is the mother who has most need of this knowledge. This is why all young girls should be obliged to spend a certain time in the practical schools I have already suggested. To be effective education should begin far earlier than is generally the case; actually in the first few weeks after birth. Limited at first to physiological training, it should extend after the end of the first year to mental formation. Time has not the same value for a child as for its parents. A day is incomparably longer at one year old than at thirty for it contains possibly six times as many physiological and mental events. This immensely rich period of infancy should not be left uncultivated. It is probably during the first six years that it is most crucial to carry out the rules of reasonable behavior. The mother plays a role of capital importance in the future of her child and hence in that of our civilization. In spite of this, democratic education gives young girls no sort of preparation for their true function in society. After the fifth or sixth year, teachers and professors share with the parents the responsibility of training the young. Hitherto they have been unsuccessful because they separate the intellectual from the physiological and the moral. One may be permitted to state that the enormous intellectual effort demanded from children during the last thirty or forty years has served no good purpose. The moral and physiological decline of youth is painfully apparent. In no other civilized country is there such a small percentage of great scientists, philanthropists and athletes relative to its population as we find in France. From the moment it goes to school, at the same time as it learns the alphabet, a child should be trained to obey the basic laws of social life. Bad manners, dirtiness, jealousy, deceitfulness and tale-telling are much more serious faults than ignorance of grammar or of geography. It is no less important to apply the rules of rational behavior than to apply those of arithmetic. The moment has come to break the old molds. The school can only contribute to the rescue of our civilization by enlarging its framework. It must abandon its purely intellectual point of view. It will be a great day when examinations stop classifying children and young people simply and solely according to their memory.

In France, the certificate of studies, the *baccalauréat* and the other public examinations take not the least account of the real worth of the candidate, for this worth is quite as much moral and psychological as intellectual. In future, diplomas ought to be awarded not merely for intellectual knowledge but also for the moral and psychological results of rational conduct.

The majority of people still do not understand the significance of the events which are disrupting the face of the earth. Often they put their hopes in the return of those conditions of life which were the real cause of their ills. They continue to live in the same delusions and in the same psychological and mental flabbiness as before. Such persistent blindness shows how far they are from realizing the urgent need to change their way of behaving.

This makes it extremely difficult for isolated individuals to live more rationally. The only resource for the nonconformists is to band together. Often two or three people can create a center from which new ideas will gradually spread. We know the immense success of the Communist cells. The conquest of a whole factory can be made by four or five men. Extremely small groups are capable of extremely powerful action. Today we ought to assemble together all those who want to rebuild themselves and to rebuild society.

Two kinds of association are possible, associations of individuals and associations of families. Associations of families would have the great advantage of furnishing children with a suitable educational background, a background which school does not succeed in giving them. Any association—political, religious, professional or sporting—can, if its members realize the necessity, become a center of human reconstruction.

What needs to be done in all civilized countries is to encourage the emergence of small cells of reasonable conduct. Little by little these cells would increase and unite with one another like the grafts of healthy skin on the surface of a great wound. It demands such enormous effort to keep strictly to the laws of life in modern society that it would be easier to make it in common. The people who are capable of doing so do not know one another. They are still separated from each other by the vast mass of the inert. The moment has come for the living to separate themselves from the dead and to act. Only those who burn with the passion for adventure are fitted to build the new City.

4 | *Goal of the Journey and Rule of the Road.—Mirages.* *—How to Define the Aim of Life Clearly.—Need of a* *Common Direction for Humanity.*

We have started on our course. But in what direction are we moving? It is not enough to know the rule of the road; we must also know where to go. We are not idly cruising along like those motorists who drive aimlessly along the highroads every Sunday.

We have undertaken a difficult journey; we can never return to our starting point. In order not to lose our way, we must not only know the rules of conduct but we must also clearly distinguish the end to be achieved. If he does not know where he is going, the finest of pilots will fly in a circle and arrive nowhere. We must know from the outset toward which airfield to direct our will when we are lost in storm, fog or darkness.

The real aim of our existence is dictated by the nature of things. It is independent of our appetites, our caprices and even of our highest aspirations. Most men dispose of their bodies and souls without asking themselves if the goal which they have arbitrarily assigned themselves is really the one which nature secretly intends. The direction of their existence is determined by the economic status of their family, by their hereditary qualities, by their mental and material milieu, by the religious doctrine or philosophical temper of their age and by their own will.

At certain moments in the history of Western civilization, men have agreed among themselves to direct their thought and their actions toward the same end.

For our ancestors in the Middle Ages, earthly existence was only the preparation for an existence outside space and time where each one would be treated according to his merits. The goal of life was thus situated beyond death. It has been brought back to this world by the moderns. Today the majority places it in obtaining the material and intellectual advantages society can procure for them with the aid of science and technology. It is a strange weakness of democratic Liberalism to teach that life has no goal fixed by the nature of things; that it has no end other than the satisfaction of our bodily and intellectual needs.

Nevertheless, there are still many men and women who pursue neither profit, security nor the exclusive satisfaction of their material needs, but a great ideal. For the poet, the craftsman and the artist this ideal is beauty; for the scientist or the religious it is truth. Those who sacrifice themselves also live for an ideal; so does the woman who gives herself entirely to the noble task of having children and bringing them up.

There is profound diversity among the objectives to which individuals devote their lives in modern society. One and all desire happiness. But, for most of us, happiness can only be obtained at other people's expense. Thus the pursuit of it has set us against each other; individuals against individuals and nations against nations. What civilized beings have, in fact, chosen as their objective in life is war.

Science has opened up to man a realm which is marvelous but full of dangers. We have been deceived by strange mirages, by those phantoms which are created by a still fragmentary and wrongly used knowledge of things. Up to now, science has not yet brought us any effective aid in conducting our lives. Instead of asking it for light, we have used it to exploit nature to our own profit. Thus it has taught us nothing about the subject of our true destiny. As a guide, it has shown itself inferior to intuition, tradition and religious revelation. We have not known how to avail ourselves of its power.

Nevertheless, it alone is capable of embracing the whole of reality accessible to man, for its jurisdiction extends to the whole domain of the observable. This domain comprises the spiritual as well as the material, for the only means of attaining the spiritual is by observation of ourselves and others. Neither our doctrines, our desires nor our dreams will reveal to us the reason and the goal of our existence. The objective of life can only be revealed by the systematic study of the living. It is in man himself that we must read his destiny just as one reads the function of a machine in the machine itself.

If Prometheus or Archimedes were to be resurrected at this moment, they would undoubtedly guess for what end such an unknown organism as an airplane had been created. The human organism, like the inanimate body of the airplane, is evidently constructed in order to function. The destiny of the airplane is to fly; the destiny of man is to live.

The end of life is not profit, amusement, philosophy, science or religion. It is not even happiness: it is life itself.

Life consists in the plenitude of all the organic and mental activities of our body. Thus it can only attain its end on condition of never reducing, atrophying, misdirecting or perverting these activities. If we really live according to the mute commands of life, we are sure of accomplishing our destiny. We take the wrong road when, as we are at liberty to do, we oppose our blind desire to the immanent order of things; when we seek in the external world what we can only find in ourselves.

The aim of life is the realization of the human archetype in every single individual. Every human being has emotional, intellectual and organic needs whose satisfaction is indispensable to the fulfillment of his destiny. The true object of society is to cater for the satisfaction of these needs. Unfortunately, under the influence of materialistic Liberalism, the democratic nations have not admitted that these needs are universal. We refuse to the vast majority conditions which are absolutely necessary for the complete development of body and soul.

Our civilization is crumbling because we have allowed two things to increase at the same time: wealth which corrupts the individual and poverty which withers and atrophies him. The first duty of society is to give each of its members the possibility of fulfilling his destiny. When it becomes incapable of performing this duty it must be transformed.

If the end of life is the same for all, the means of attaining it vary according to each indiviual. No human being is identical with another. We must, therefore, find out to which type we belong; what are our physiological and psychic aptitudes and deficiencies; how we can use our good qualities and combat our vices. Then only shall we be able to choose the mode of travel which suits us. Even if one has neither airplane, motorcar nor railway at one's disposition, it is still possible to reach one's destination on horseback or on foot. Life offers itself equally to the small and the great, the weak and the strong.

Our destiny is as immutable as the structure of the universe. It is far more important for us to know this destiny than to know the topography of Alaska or the constitution of the nucleus of the atom. The goal toward which life tends is spirit, that is to say the emergence of reason and love in ourselves and in the terrestrial world. Today the whole of humanity needs to raise its eyes toward the same heaven and to set out on the same road. Otherwise, it will founder in chaos. As long as men devote their lives to a false objective they will remain incapable of mutual understanding and will destroy each other.

5 | *Meaning of Life.—Why Live?—Science Remains Mute.—The Answer of Religion.—Necessity for Working Hypotheses.—What Are We?*

Like the monkey, man is characterized by an insatiable curiosity. Thus he is incessantly trying to solve insoluble problems. It is not enough for him to know that the goal of life is life itself, that in harmoniously developing his physical and mental activities according to natural laws he is fully accomplishing his destiny; he insists on asking as well what is the meaning of life. Why are we here? Where do we come from? What are we? What is the place of intelligence in the universe? Why so much suffering, anxiety and trouble? What is the meaning of death? What is the point of modeling body and soul according to an ideal of goodness and truth if we are soon to revert to nothing? Are not enthusiasm, faith and heroism mere jests on the part of nature? Where are we going? After death, does the spirit disintegrate like the body? Is it absurd to believe in the survival of the soul?

Today, as in all times and in all countries, there exist men and women to whom mere living does not seem enough. Life does not appear to them as the most precious of all goods. They thirst after beauty, renunciation and love. They want to attain to God.

To the questions of such people, philosophy has never given more than anemic answers. Neither Socrates nor Plato has succeeded in calming the anguish of humanity faced with the mystery of life.

Only religion proposes a complete solution to the human problem. Christianity, above all has given a clear-cut answer to the demands of the human soul. For centuries it has calmed the restless curiosity which men have always felt concerning their destiny. Religious inspiration, divine revelation and faith brought certainty and peace to our forefathers.

But reason intensified its eternal warfare against intuition. Under the blows of the philosophers of the Age of Enlightenment, particularly of Voltaire and the Encyclopedists, religion lost ground. Science brought man a form of certainty different from that of faith; simple, clear, easily demonstrable truths which could often be expressed in concise and elegant mathematical formulas. Religion, on the contrary, continued to employ the concepts and the language of the Middle Ages. Today at least three-quarters of the inhabitants of Europe and the United States no longer demand from Christianity the solution of the disturbing problem of our nature and our destiny.

Here we can hope for no help from science. Science is

content to transmit to us the orders given by nature to live, to reproduce our kind and to develop our spirit. She shows us the end of life but she remains mute concerning its meaning. She is too young to answer the questions which thinking humanity asks so anxiously when confronted with the mystery of its origin and its end. Science does not yet know the nature of spirit.[2]

All that she does know is that our personality depends simultaneously on the brain, the organs and the blood. All human activity is, as we know, at once organic and psychic. But we are totally ignorant of the relations between the cerebral processes and thought. Are we to consider the mental as identical with the cerebral or as surpassing it? Is spirit produced by living matter or is it only located in it? These questions still remain unanswered.

Nevertheless, the astronomers of Mount Wilson have succeeded in photographing the gigantic nebulæ which are 500 million light years distant from the earth. In spite of its resistance, modern physicists have forced the nucleus of the atom to reveal the secret of its constitution. At the same time the geneticists of the school of Morgan have discovered in the chromosomes of the sexual cells structural unities, as impressive as those of the atoms, which are the seat of the hereditary potentialities of body and mind. But no one yet knows the function of the delicate organs which Ramon y Cajal was the first to observe in the brain cells nor the relations of these cells to thought. All that we know is that the characteristics of the personality depend on certain conditions of the glandular and nervous systems.

This being, at once familiar and unknown, which is ourself still remains inaccessible to scientific techniques. Is it then unknowable? Or could it be apprehended by far subtler and more searching methods than any we have today?

[2] *Man the Unknown.*

We have no idea. Before any question touching the origin, the nature or the destiny of the spirit, science maintains a complete silence.

It is, however, permissible to make certain hypotheses about this subject. Hypotheses are indeed indispensable to the progress of knowledge for their verification stimulates the invention of new techniques and the institution of new experiments. It matters little whether a hypothesis be true or false; its function is merely to force use to set to work. Consequently a hypothesis which does not lead to any observation or to any new experiment is only a vain supposition. It is idle, for example, to discuss the origin of life or of consciousness for these phenomena have had no witness; their history will never be revealed to us and any hypothesis concerning them will remain barren.

On the contrary, the suppositions which we can make concerning the nature and the future of spirit are capable of engendering fresh research. They would, therefore, be fertile even if they were later invalidated by fact.

When he embarked on the Great Lakes, Père Marquette believed that he was setting out for China. Nevertheless, this false hypothesis was useful; if he did not arrive in China, he did at least found Chicago.

What are we? We know already that we are autonomous and conscious bodies which move freely on the surface of the earth. Each one of these bodies is composed of cells, liquids and spirit. It has certain characteristics which differentiate it from all other bodies and it has a distinct personality. Its spatial limits are well defined and yet it can pass beyond these limits and change the properties of the space which surrounds it.[3] For it creates round about it a field or force which exerts its influence on all the animate and inanimate beings which come within it.

[3] *Ibid.*

Men mutually repel or attract each other. There are invisible bonds between them which unite members of the same community like a network. It is thought which has transformed the terrestrial world and the conditions of life. We know, too, that the possession of this spiritual energy constitutes our peculiar character. It essentially differentiates us from our nearest relatives in the animal kingdom, the anthropoid apes and, in particular, the chimpanzees. Spirit appears in living matter when the brain and the endocrine glands attain a certain degree of perfection. Like the phosphorescence of the glowworm, it is a kind of light emitted by living tissues.

What is the structure of thought? Do there exist psychons analogous to the photons of a sunbeam or to the electrons and protons of electric fluid? Or are we dealing with a completely new world which our present concepts are impotent to describe? The study of consciousness undoubtedly reserves still greater surprises for the biologists of the future than those which the exploration of the interatomic world has provided for the physiologists.

The spirit forms part of the body and is, therefore, situated in the physical continuum. But it escapes from the four dimensions of space and time just as the light does not remain imprisoned in the bulb of a lamp. Spiritual energy presents characteristics which vary according to individuals. These characteristics are transmitted hereditarily. There are factors in the genes which determine, though in what measure we do not yet know, the quality of the spirit. The spirit, like the secretion of the gastric juices of thyroxin, depends, therefore, on the activity of certain groups of cells and yet it does not belong to the same world as these cells. Is it the smoke produced by the burning wood or is it the cloud which hovers for a moment in the pine forest on the side of the mountain?

We are neither spirit nor body, for spirit and body only constitute complementary aspects of ourselves. The structure of our senses does not permit us to apprehend both these aspects simultaneously. No mental activity is ever produced without the corresponding organic activity.

Spirit, as we know, presents different types in different individuals. There are, for example, intellectual, affective and intuitive types. Each of these types is characterized by the predominance of one or other of the physicomental activities.

The human person is constituted, first and foremost, by consciousness. But consciousness is simultaneously linked to the brain, the blood, the endocrine glands, the sympathetic nervous system and the heart. The unity of the eye, like the unity of the organism, consists of multiple elements. We are intelligence, feeling and intuition just as much as we are pituitary, suprarenal, thyroid and sexual glands, cerebral cortex and hypothalamus. It is an error to believe that the brain is the seat of the intelligence. The truth is, we think with all our organs but it is probable that the power of understanding, remembering and associating ideas depends on the number of nerve cells, the perfection of their structure and the complexity of their system of association. The intellect uses the information which the sense organs give it about the external world and prepares our action on this world. Thanks to its inventions, it has enormously increased the acuteness of our preceptions and the power of our hands. It has constructed the gigantic telescopes of California and Mount Wilson which can reach universes situated several million light years from our Milky Way. It has also invented the electronic microscope which is strong enough to let us penetrate into the world of molecules. It has given us the means of acting on the greatest as well as the smallest objects; of destroying in a few minutes monuments which were the glory of our civilization; of performing surgical operations on isolated cells or of splitting the nucleus of the atom. The intellect is the creator of science and philosophy. When it is well balanced, it constitutes a sure guide to conduct but it gives us neither the sense of life nor the strength to live. It is only one of the activities of the spirit. If it developes in isolation, unaccompanied by feeling, it separates an individual from other individuals and dehumanizes him.

Feeling depends more on the endocrine glands, the sympathetic nervous system and the heart than on the brain. Enthusiasm, courage, love and hate impel us to the action which the intelligence has planned. It is fear, anger, the passion to discover and to dare which act, through the medium of the sympathetic nerves, on the glands whose secretions put the organism in a state to act, to defend itself, to run away or to attack. The pituitary, thyroid, sexual and suprarenal glands render love, hate, enthusiasm and faith possible. It is only thanks to these organs that human associations can exist. Reason alone is impotent to unite individuals. It is capable neither of loving nor hating. The Christian virtues are more difficult to practice when our endocrine glands are deficient.

Feeling apprehends reality in a more direct way than does intelligence. Intelligence considers life from the outside; feeling dwells in the inmost core of life. The heart has its reasons which reason does not know, as Pascal said. It is these nonintellectual activities of the spirit which give an individual the power to come out of himself, to make contact with others, to love them and to sacrifice himself for them.

Perhaps artistic inspiration, religious inspiration and love favor the development of intuition. The poet apprehends reality in a deeper way than the scientist. Intuition comes very close to clairvoyance; it appears to be the extrasensorial perception of reality. "All great men are gifted with intuition. They know without reasoning or analysis, what they need to know." [4]

It is probable that the difference between intuition and clairvoyance is quantitative and qualitative. "Clairvoyance and telepathy are immediate data of observation. Those who have this power grasp the secret thoughts of other individuals without using their sense organs. They also perceive events which are more or less distant in space or time." This gift is far from being exceptional. In his researches on the students of Duke University, Rhine frequently observed the existence of extrasensorial perception. The prophets of the Old Testament knew the future. In the eleventh century, the Arabs defined extrasensorial perception as the fourth degree of mental development. The doctrine of Yoga teaches that the transmission of thought from one person to another is possible. Fichte, Hegel, Schopenhauer and von Hauptman admitted the concept of extrasensorial perception. Strangely enough, Aristotle rejected divination, for this phenomenon seemed to him inexplicable. Descartes and the eighteenth century philosophers also believed that nothing can penetrate to the intelligence except through the senses.

Thus, since the Renaissance, man has been arbitrarily imprisoned within the frontiers of his five senses. Today we know many undeniable cases of telepathy. The nature of telepathy, of the vision of the past and of the prediction of the future, remains as unknown as in Aristotle's time. But we do know that we must never deny the reality of a phenomenon simply because this phenomenon is inexplicable and difficult to observe.

It is certain that the spirit can communicate with the external world and with other spirits through some other

[4] *Ibid.*

channel than the sense organs. Undoubtedly intuition is far from being as solid as intellect. Its use is frequently dangerous. But this extrasensorial perception greatly increases our spirit's power of penetration for it allows us to grasp things beyond the reach of our senses in space and time and even perhaps beyond them both.

Man is thus constructed in such a way as to be aware of purely spiritual influences, whether it is a question of the unexpressed thought of another man or of the grace of God. Aristotle, St. Thomas Aquinas, Descartes and his disciples have made the existence of all revealed religion conceivable. There are, in fact, far wider contacts between ourselves and external or internal reality than classical philosophy and science recognize. We live at once in space and time and outside these dimensions of the physical universe. We have at our disposition, not only the force of the intellect but that of intuition or clairvoyance. The intellect gives us knowledge and mastery of the material world. Intuition penetrates deeper than intelligence into reality and unites us directly with things. It is above all due to these nonintellectual activities that the spirit can escape beyond the material world. This property of the physicomental substance of being able to inhabit simultaneously the physical universe and a universe inaccessible, at any rate for the moment, to reason and science, makes the human being an object different from anything else which exists in the terrestrial world. That is what we are.

6 | *Position of Man in the Universe.—Is He the Only Thinking Being?—Psychic Aspect of the Cosmos.—Belief in Exclusively Spiritual Entities.—The Hypothesis of God.*

Each individual thinks himself the center of the world. Nothing seems more important to us than our own existence. We have the feeling that our life has a profound significance. Is this feeling a mere illusion, a device of nature to oblige us to obey the law of the conservation of life? What is our real position in the universe?

Certainly we are the masters of the earth. But the earth is only one of the planets which turn round the sun. And the sun is only a tiny star among the millions of stars which make up the Milky Way of which it is part. And beyond the Milky Way there are many other universes; floating islands in the vastness of space. The telescope at Mount Wilson has deciphered such universes at a distance of more than 400 million light years. Obviously, from the quantitative point of view, the presence of man in the universe is completely negligible. But the value of a thing does not depend on its size or its weight. A watch, for example, differs from a pebble of the same weight. The Venus of Milo is something more than a block of marble of the same dimensions still lying in the quarry.

Compared to the vertiginous grandeur of the sidereal world or even compared to our own small earth, the brain of man is something infinitesimally small. Nevertheless, it is of an incomparable quality. This harmonious association of more than twelve thousand million nervous cells, bound to each other several trillions of times by delicate fibrils, has no equal in the cosmic world. From this infinitesimal quantity of living matter springs the immense force of thought. Thought not only encompasses the whole material universe from the vast nebulæ to the nuclei of atoms but extends far beyond it. The human being has incomparably greater value than the huge inanimate mass of the cosmic world. Nowhere else is such structural perfection found. Perhaps the brain is the one single point in the universe where the conditions indispensable to the emergence of spirit from matter are to be found.

Does thinking matter exist only on the earth, to the exclusion of the planets which possibly revolve about innumerable other suns? It is highly improbable that spirit should only have manifested itself on this microscopical point of the sidereal universe. Nevertheless, the physical and chemical conditions necessary to life as we know it are complex. They are not generally to be found in planets other than the earth. The moon has neither water nor atmosphere; a telescope reveals no sign of vegetation. The atmosphere of Venus contains much carbonic anhydride but neither water vapor nor oxygen. The climate of Mars is temperate; its atmosphere contains oxygen, carbonic anhydride and water vapor: the seasonal changes in the color of certain regions of the planet indicate the presence of abundant vegetation. In the solar system, life is only possible on the earth and on Mars. Are there no other worlds which might be habitable for beings like ourselves?

We know that planets are produced when two stars approach each other so close that satellites are formed by their mutual attraction. Perhaps our humble planet really has that privileged position in the universe which the astronomers, philosophers and theologians of the Middle Ages attributed to it before Copernicus. According to Eddington, over a period of ten thousand million years, only one star among a hundred million other stars has sustained such an encounter. Thus, since planetary systems are extremely rare, it is possible that there exists no other human race.

In the cosmos, spirit is not found outside living matter. Yet all the elements which make up the bodies of men and animals are furnished by earth, water and air. Does spirit also come from these elements? Is it born when certain chemical reactions take place? Does the cosmic world contain psychic elements of which we are ignorant just as we were ignorant of the cosmic rays until the invention of a technique which discovered them?

At this moment, we have no conception how chemical reactions and physiological processes can bring about the development of the human person. We may, however, allow ourselves to suppose that the external environment contains diffused psychic energy, either free or united to inert matter. This energy would enter into the composition of the body and principally of the brain and there personify itself. But if such spiritual energy existed in the physical world which surrounds us, we should not be capable of detecting its presence. Just as we are incapable of establishing the existence of mental processes when we observe the brain of an unanesthetized patient during an operation, so is it impossible for our sense organs to apprehend spirit directly.

Man has always refused to believe that he was the only thinking being on earth. Our ancestors believed in the existence of spiritual entities who inhabited their houses as well as river, mountains and forests. The cities of antiquity were founded on religion, that is to say on certain obligations which linked men with invisible spirits. Extremely detailed techniques were elaborated to render these spirits favorable. The dead consented to return among their relatives and friends and sometimes gave them useful advice. Laws, too, were inspired from on high; was not the constitution of Sparta revealed to Lycurgus by Apollo?

Later, Christianity purified these beliefs. Angels and saints replaced the little domestic gods. During the Middle Ages the humblest peasant lived in the company of spiritual beings. In the solitude of the fields or forests, he was never alone. It was St. Michael, St. Catherine and St. Margaret who gave Joan of Arc her mission. Each one could live his life in the company of God and His saints and receive from them inner strength and peace. The Mother of God blessed innumerable places with her presence: for example, the grotto on the bank of the Gave near the village of Lourdes.

Later still, industrial civilization developed. The Calvaries which stood at the crossroads and the chapels in the fields were little by little abandoned by their divine guests. Even the spirits which were sometimes met after sunset near old wells and deserted farms vanished, never to return.

As a result, modern men reverted to the customs of their pagan ancestors. Once again they attempted to communicate with the dead. For the saints and the angels they substituted vague spiritual entities: disembodied souls and psychic factors which, with the help of mediums and automatic writing, brought us singularly uninteresting information about the beyond.

Today, as in other ages, man seeks the company of invisible beings capable of helping, loving and protecting him. But he knows that these spiritual entities are beyond his reach. Only the great intuitives and the clairvoyants may perceive their presence and communicate with them.

If inanimate matter contains psychic elements, we shall always remain ignorant of them. Nevertheless, the cosmos carries, as it were, the imprint of a spirit which our own spirit resembles in certain aspects.

There is, as we know, an evident order in the universe.

It is an order we are capable of understanding. Even the mathematical abstractions constructed by our mind express almost exactly the ways in which the world about us behaves. There must be, then, some resemblance between our reason and that which appears to have created the world. This creative reason, this God, appears to us to treat inanimate matter as a mathematician would do. This God of our mind remains very far away from us. Inexorable as the law of gravity, inaccessible as the sun, He only bends down to great geniuses such as Newton, Ampère, Planck and Broglie. But, when He concerns Himself with animate matter, He loses the simplicity of His method and His triumphant logic. The evolution of living beings seems to us to have been directed by a clumsy, wasteful, brutal and vacillating, though obstinate force toward a definite end which is the rise of spirit. All along the road there have opened up innumerable impasses into which life has strayed as if by mistake. Only at the price of ambiguous and complicated maneuvers, only after a very long and frequently misdirected effort does Nature, or the Will of God, seem to us to have realized the human being.

The hypothesis of God, wrote Arthur H. Campton, gives a more reasonable interpretation of the universe than any other hypothesis. It is quite as legitimate as many of the hypotheses of physics and its fertility has already been immense. There is no reason for rejecting it. Millikan, Eddington and Jeans believe, like Newton, that the cosmos is the product of a creative intelligence. But this hypothesis which satisfies physicists and astronomers, is not sufficient for the man in the street. This God of Newton does not concern himself with our joys, sorrows and anxieties any more than does the God of Plato. We do not want to have for God a mathematician or a cruel and clumsy experimenter. We need a God who loves us, hears us and helps us.

7 | *The Need of God.—Prayer.—The Mystical Experi-ence.—Its Significance.—Liberalism and Religion.—Nature of Reality.*

For nearly two centuries, religion has been gradually replaced by the worship of profit and the worship of science. In France it has been banished from the state schools. In modern society, it is practically ignored. But, in spite of the disfavor into which it has fallen, it is far from being dead.

Man continues his eternal pursuit of the spiritual substratum of things. In all ages and in nearly all countries, he has felt the need to adore. The tendency to adore is almost as natural to him as the tendency to love. This search for God is probably a necessary consequence of the structure of our mind. In the carpenter of Nazareth, man has found the God at once sublime and familiar who suits his needs. The words of Jesus penetrate deeply into the reality of life. They ignore philosophy; they break all the conventions; they are so astonishing that, even to this day, we find them hard to understand.

We are, after all, near relatives of the gorillas and the Sermon on the Mount shocks certain of our hereditary tendencies. To him who obeys the law of the jungle, the command to love his neighbor as himself seems absurd.

Nevertheless, Jesus knows our world. He does not disdain us like the God of Aristotle. We can speak to Him and He answers us. Although He is a person like ourselves, He is God and transcends all things. But we can also encounter Him acting in the wood of the table, in the food we eat, in the sunbeam which warms us, in earth, sky and air, because He has created and conserves all things. Wherever we are, at any moment of day or night, He is at our disposition. We can reach Him simply by turning toward Him our desire and our love. It is an easily observable fact that, even in the society created by science and technology, this need of God has persisted, in a more or less definite form, in a large number of individuals. When it is not satisfied it often, like the sexual instinct, becomes perverted. Its persistence in surviving even in the most unfavorable conditions shows that it would be dangerous to ignore it.

The need of God expresses itself in prayer. Prayer is a cry of distress; a demand for help; a hymn of love. It does not consist in the dreary recitation of words whose sense we do not understand. Its effect is nearly always positive. Everything happens as if God listened to us and gave us a direct answer; unexpected events occur; mental balance is reestablished; our sense of isolation and impotence and of the uselessness of our efforts disappears. The world ceases to be cruel and unjust and becomes friendly while a strange power develops in our own depths.

Prayer gives us strength to bear cares and anxieties, to hope when there is no logical motive for hope, to remain steadfast in the midst of catastrophes. These phenomena can occur in everyone but most of all in those who shut out the tumult and confusion of modern life from their souls. The world of science is different from the world of prayer. But it is not opposed to it any more than the rational is opposed to the nonrational. We must never forget that spirit is composed both of logical and nonlogical activities. The results of prayer are relevant to science as well as to religion. Prayer acts not only on our affective states but also on the physiological processes. Sometimes it cures organic diseases in a few instants or a few days. However incomprehensible these phenomena may be, we are forced to admit their reality. The Bureau of Medical Testimony at Lourdes has registered more than two hundred cases of tuberculosis, blindness or osteomyelitis, cancer and other organic diseases whose almost instantaneous cure is undisputed. Here we are on solid ground. Man needs help: he prays; the help comes. Whatever its future interpretation may be, this fact remains eternally true.

Knowledge of the material world comes to us through the combined efforts of theory and experiment. Thanks to experimental techniques, we have discovered and analyzed a great number of physical phenomena. Subsequently, theory has gathered these facts into a coherent system, foreseen new facts and inspired new experiments. In the same way the knowledge of the spiritual substratum also depends on theory and experiment, that is to say on mysticism and theology. Mysticism is, as we know, the essence of religion. The mystical experience differs as profoundly from philosophical knowledge as love differs from reason. Moreover, it always remains true whereas philosophical knowledge changes just as physical theories have changed and will change again.

Great mystics are as rare as great scientists. The birth of St. Paul was an even more exceptional event than the birth of Newton or Pasteur. The experimental search for God demands long and hard labor.[5] No one can engage in the mystical way without first submitting himself to the rigors of the purgative life, purifying his senses and practicing the Christian virtues. Only then can begin the journey whose end is union with God. This union is not intellectual for God always remains indescribable and unknowable. Nevertheless, the apprehension of God by feeling is so strong, evident and immediate that it gives the contemplative complete certainty of its reality. The God thus discovered is Love and not Reason. The dark night which must be tra-

[5] *Man the Unknown.*

versed before attaining Him appears indeed to be a suspension of the activities of the senses and the reason. One might say that man only attains to God after having extinguished the images of the world in himself and momentarily arrested his intellectual processes. The mystical experience confirms and extends the deductions of theology; it reinforces the traditional teaching of the Church; it is an attestation of the value of religion.

Must we ask ourselves if "the mystical experience is true or false, whether it is auto-suggestion or hallucination or whether indeed it represents the soul's journey beyond the dimension of our world and its contact with a higher reality"? Perhaps it would be wiser to be content to have an operational concept of it and to accept the gifts it brings us without searching for their origin. But we want to know whether the mystics really attain to God and if their experience conforms to the order of things. God, by definition, is an immateral being. He cannot be seen, heard, smelled, tasted or touched. God, if one accepts Aristotle's teaching, is therefore beyond man's reach. But our science is more extensive than Aristotle's. Nowadays we admit the existence of extrasensorial perception. We know too that this phenomenon is more likely to occur when intellectual activity is suspended. Experienced clairvoyants have learned to make their minds a blank. The night of the intelligence, described by Ruysbroek, and the ecstasy of St. Theresa of Avila have a striking analogy with the mental void favorable to telepathic phenomena. Moreover, the clairvoyant experiences, like the mystic, the absolute certainty of having attained his object. In both cases this certitude cannot be shaken by any argument. There is, thus, a certain analogy between the mystical experience and the extrasensorial perception of thought. Is it more extraordinary to communicate with God than with a human being more or less remote from us in space or time? Even though it is not scientifically proved that the mystic does attain God, it would be absurd not to attribute a profound significance to religious experience.

The existence of God explains, better than any other hypothesis, the results of prayer, the phenomena of mysticism and the sense of the holy. It is prudent to consider the need of the divine, not as illusory, but as the expression of structural characteristics of the human spirit which are more or less developed according to the individual. Since the universe is a coherent system, the fact of there being such a need makes us anticipate a means of satisfying it in the external world. For example, the cells of the organism would not be aerobic if there were no oxygen in the atmosphere. Equally, the need of water, fat, sugar or protein implies the existence of these substances in the external environment. It is permissible to attribute the same significance to a more or less obscure need felt by a great number of human beings to communicate with an invisible and sovereignly powerful Spirit; a Spirit at once personal and immanent in all things, which is manifested to us through intuition, revelation and the natural laws.

It is a strange fact that modern man has eliminated all psychic factors from reality. He has built himself up an environment which is exclusively material. This world does not suit him and he is degenerating in it. For thousands of years our ancestors considered the presence of spiritual elements in their environment as essential. Above the village rose the church spire. Religion presided over the important events of life—birth, marriage and death; it gave each person the courage to live. It seemed evident that if it is to avoid a definite collapse into chaos and incoherence, civilized humanity must once again build cathedrals in the bleakly magnificent universe of the physicists and the astronomers.

It is not a question of putting back the clock, of reviving

the age of St. Thomas Aquinas or of Chartres cathedral. Nor is it a question of confining ourselves to the universe of Einstein, Shapley or Broglie. In spite of its vastness, this universe embraces only part of reality, for the human intelligence which created it has reserved no place in it for itself. Yet the world of lovers, artists and mystics is quite as real as that of engineers, scientists and philosophers. Art, morality and religion are no less indispensable than science. The modern universe, as conceived by Liberalism or Marxism, is too tight a garment. It would be absurd if external reality were incapable of encompassing man in his totality. It would also be absurd if its structure did not correspond in some measure to our own. It is thus reasonable to attribute the same objectivity to the world of spirit as to the world of matter.

8 | *Where Are We Going?—Significance of Death.—Dissolution, Temporary Survival or Immortality?— Answer of Science.—Answer of Religion.—Opposition of Science and Feeling.—What Life Ordains.—The Choice of a Hypothesis.*

Where are we going? Toward death. Even if we came to the point, thanks to new discoveries, of reversing the direction of physiological time, of periodically rejuvenating ourselves and even of prolonging our lives for two or three centuries, death would not be overcome because the structure of our body makes death a necessity. From the very inception of its existence in the womb, the young organism begins to age. This process of senescence is much more rapid in the fetus and the young child than in the adult and still more than in the old. The progress toward death slows down considerably with advancing years but it never stops and never changes its direction. Whatever the future successes of science may be, every human being is condemned sooner or later to disappear from this world.

What is the significance of death? We know very well what our body will become, some gases and a handful of ashes. And our spirit? It appears to be annihilated at the same time as the organs. Since, during life, it is inseparable from the tissues and the blood, it is logical to think that it decomposes when they do. Nevertheless, feeling has always refused to accept this verdict of reason.

Men of the West ardently desire life, not only in this world but also beyond the tomb. It is not enough for them to survive in their works, in the trees they have planted and the houses they have built, in the inventions of their brain, in the immediate or remote consequences of their actions. Neither are they content to perpetuate themselves in their descendants through the medium of the genes which they themselves received from their ancestors. What we desire above all is personal survival. We long to see, after death, those whom we love; we long to enter into the realm of justice and peace and to enjoy the ineffable companionship of God.

The peoples who have succeeded each other on the earth have nearly always believed in at least the temporary survival of the spirit. The Church has even elevated belief in the immortality of the soul and the resurrection of the body to the rank of a dogma. Though the majority of civilized people have abandoned religious faith, many of them still ponder deeply on the mystery of death. They ask themselves anxiously whether spiritual development is truly the aim of life; whether the spiritual treasures accumulated by the heroes of charity and by the saints are inevitably doomed to be swallowed up in nothingness. To these questions science can, at the moment, give no answer. It is still ignorant of the relations between the mental and the cerebral; nor can it say whether the dissolution of the cerebral necessarily entails that of the mental. It is equally ignorant of the nature of spirit. Perhaps this ignorance will be permanent for spirit, though involved in living matter, is beyond the spatio-temporal world and hence beyond the jurisdiction of science. Even if disembodied souls were pullulating all about us, we should not know it for we possess no means of ascertaining their presence.

What, then, do apparitions of the dead signify? There exists a large number of undoubtedly authentic cases where a deceased person has appeared to a relative or friend at the moment of their death, or very shortly after, and has told them in what circumstances it took place. Thanks to automatic writing or through the channel of a medium, alleged communications come to us from beyond. These messages usually deal with the unverifiable conditions of the life of disembodied spirits. But sometimes they contain a surprising revelation of things known only to the deceased person. Sir Oliver Lodge always believed that he was in communication with his son for several years after the latter's death. Spiritualists teach that messages thus received are a proof of the survival of the spirit. They believe that, if not the whole consciousness, at least a psychic principle persists after death. This principle unites itself with the spirit of the medium and constitutes a kind of consciousness belonging at once to the medium and to the dead person. Its existence seems to be transitory. It gradually disintegrates and finally disappears.

The importance of the facts on which these speculations are based is undeniable, but their interpretation is certainly not correct for the spiritualists leave clairvoyance out of account. Yet we know that clairvoyants perceive past events as well as future ones. For them there is no secret. The revelations attributed to the spirit of the dead person may merely be due to the clairvoyance of the medium. We cannot distinguish a phenomenon of survival from a phenomenon of clairvoyance so that, for the moment, we have no scientific proof that the spirit survives death. Nevertheless, no one can definitely state that such a science is impossible. The systematic study of metapsychical phenomena will no doubt help us to know the properties of spirit just as pathological phenomena have given us a better understanding of the physiology of the nervous system. Unfortunately, this study is discredited by the charlatans who claim to deal with it. The moment has come for science to venture into the *terræ incognitæ* whose discovery may perhaps throw some light on the nature of the spirit.

Religion gives a very different interpretation of death from that of science. For religion, death represents not the end of life but its beginning. Instead of dissolving at the same time as the body, the spirit continues its ascent and, without losing its personality, is absorbed in God.

For the last two thousand years, hundreds of millions of men and women have died at peace, with the certitude of living an after-life with their dear ones, with the saints and angels and with God Himself. The mystics who have succeeded in crossing the threshold of the unitive life experience, even in this world, the indescribable joy of contact with God which the beatific vision will give eternally to the elect after death.

The Church promises man not only the immortality of his body and soul but also, if he is worthy, the possession of God and endless happiness. Thus the answer of faith to humanity's anguish when confronted with the mystery of death is incomparably more satisfying than that of science. When feeling takes the form of intuition and love, it discovers what remains hidden to the intellect. "Thou wouldst not seek Me if thou hadst not already found Me," says the mystic. Religion brings man the answer which his heart desires.

Ought we to accept the answer of science or that of religion? Should we let ourselves be guided by reason or feeling? Some men obey feeling, others reason. Wisdom consists in conforming one's conduct both to reason and to feeling, to science as well as to faith, to the true as well as the beautiful. It is impossible for us to refuse to think about the significance of death. Two hypotheses present themselves. Either we completely dissolve when we die or else something of us survives. "We are embarked," as Pascal said. We have to choose. Between two working hypotheses we must choose the more audacious, the one which can lead to the greater results even if it is not the more rationally certain. We must, therefore, adopt the hypothesis of immortality though only on condition that the adoption of this hypothesis does not prevent us from obeying the laws of life. We must never forget that our evident *raison d'être*, the imperative order of nature and the aim of our existence, is to live in the fullness of our physiological and mental activities.

Is belief in immortality opposed to the laws which are inscribed in our body and our soul? Is it an encouragement or an obstacle to the preservation of life, to its propagation and the advance of spirit? Obviously, faith in the survival of the personality can only incite us to develop our consciousness in the course of our lifetime. It definitely favors spiritual advance. A very high degree of spirituality is frequently observable in those who devote their lives simultaneously to the service of others and to that of God. It is also true that, all too often, a misunderstood asceticism separates the progress of the spirit from that of the body. Consciousness cannot, in fact, attain its finest development without a corresponding organic development. To prepare the spirit for its meeting with God, the body is indispensable. Furthermore, obedience to the laws of life becomes a sacred duty. For the mystic, the laws of life are the very expression of the will of God.

Although reason considers the total dissolution of our being at the moment of death as more likely than the survival of the spirit, it cannot accept the hypothesis of immortality otherwise than favorably. The annihilation of consciousness would be just as inexplicable as its persistence. If our personality is to disappear at the same time as the body, what is the use of this spiritual development which nature seems to assign as one of the objects of individual existence? Individual existence is not directed only by the propagation of the species. For the spiritual personality continues to develop long after the time when man, and particularly woman, have lost their powers of reproduction. The evolution of the individual, like that of the race, would be a mere jest on the part of nature. The huge effort of spiritualization which living matter has accomplished over untold ages would have no sense if man's soul is destroyed at the same time as his body.

All the same, we are still no nearer to understanding how the spirit which is inseparable from the body can exist without it. Perhaps thousands of years will go by before the secret of this riddle is revealed to us. Meanwhile we may be allowed, perhaps, to consider spirit as an emanation of the brain analogous to the light produced by the tungsten filament in an electric bulb. The light is born in the filament as though in the brain but the photons of which it is composed escape from the lamp and set off on an unending journey through space. When the lamp is extinguished, the photons it has emitted do not perish. Astronomers in Cali-

fornia register photographically the arrival of photons
emitted by stars which have been dead for perhaps four
hundred million light years. It is not absurd to believe that
the spiritual energy radiated by the brain into regions situated beyond time and space continue its existence in this
unknown world after our death.

Death has a different significance for every human being
for death depends on life and the meaning of life varies
according to individuals. Nearly always, death is like the
end of a sad monotonous rainy day. Sometimes it has the
beauty of twilight in the mountains or it resembles the
sleep of a hero after the fight. But it can be, if we so desire,
the immersion of the soul in the splendor of God.

9 | *Influence of Rational Conduct on Life.—From I to
We.—The Four Types of Union with Another.—
Increasing the Aptitude for Union.—The Social
Value of the Individual.*

Every individual who behaves in a rational way gradually
undergoes a profound transformation. When body and spirit
act as their constitution ordains, they become more efficient.
This progress is marked, above all, by the development of
character, moral sense, intuition, sense of the holy and capacity for love and self-sacrifice. Intelligence becomes more
acute. When man understands that the aim of life is not
material profit but life itself, he ceases to fix his attention
exclusively on the external world. He considers more atten-
tively his own existence and the existence of those around
him. He realizes that he depends on others and that others
depend on him; that, in the human race, male and female
are mentally complementary just as their sexual organs are

complementary; that the slow development of the young and their psychological frailty demand community life. Thus we perceive the artificiality of Rousseau's conventions, the absurdity of the social contract and the danger of individualism. We become aware of the necessity of considering others as much as ourselves in every circumstance of life.

There is an obvious antagonism between the egoism indispensable to individual survival and the altruism demanded by social life. The organism is formed and grows at the expense of its environment and of other human beings. During its life in the womb, it is a parasite on its mother; until it becomes adult, it is a parasite on the family and on the community. It thus becomes accustomed to consider the exploitation of everything about it to its own profit as a right. The success of individualism comes from this innate tendency to egoism which characterizes every living being. On the other hand, egoism carried to excess makes any authentic community impossible. Altruism, therefore, is quite as necessary as egoism. Between these two opposing tendencies, I and We, a balance must be achieved; a balance which is indispensable to the success of our personal life. In the same way the precision of the movements of the hand come from the antagonism between the extensor and the flexor muscles of the fingers. "I" is transformed into "We" in many different ways.

The capacity for union varies in different individuals. It depends on our inherited potentialities and, above all, on the education and the mental climate of the country and the age in which we live. It is almost nonexistent in the modern Frenchman; much greater in the German and the American. In the first centuries of the Church, at the time of the persecutions, Christian communities constituted real fraternities. They were governed by mutual love and the union thus realized was indestructible and continued beyond death. Nowadays, a Catholic parish is no more than a group of people associated because of their similarity but in no way bound together by love. The capacity for union comes from the capacity to understand and to feel. The field of force which surrounds each individual can be either small or great. "We" has more or less cohesion according to the relation it implies between "I" and "Thou." "To Thee," "With Thee" and "For Thee" express quite different attitudes to one's neighbor. Materialistic Liberalism, individualism and biological morality are incapable of making progress from solidarity to love. Only by putting into practice the rules of conduct deduced from the laws of life can man increase his capacity for union with other men and establish the sharing of his own consciousness with the consciousness of others on the basis of love.

It is, above all, on his capacity for union with others that the social value of the individual depends. The discord which reigns in the family and in every aspect of our French national life comes from our ignorance of the basic necessities of communal living and our impotence to supply them. To build a house we need not only solid stones, properly shaped and adapted to each other, but also cement. Obedience to the laws of life prevents the excesses of individualism which incessantly set man against man. It represses egoism, jealousy, lying and duplicity and shows the danger of bad manners, touchiness, bad temper and lack of consideration for other people's feelings. It eliminates the personal asperities and vices which militate against the cohesion of the group and tends to unite us to each other by courtesy, generosity, kindness, love and unselfishness. Every individual who thoroughly understands the needs of our nature realizes that his personal happiness and the happiness of his children depend on his capacity to conform to the order of things. Certainly we must know how to fight.

Hitherto, fighting has been a condition of life, but war inevitably engenders war. We must also know how to forgive
our enemies, unite ourselves to them and love them.

	Man's Rights and His Needs.—Real and Artificial
10	*Needs.—Organismic Associations.—Organic Associa-*
	tions.—Transformation of Collective Life.

The human community is composed of the living, the dead
and those still unborn. Each should have a place, for the
individual is part of the community, not in virtue of any
contract, but by the mere fact of birth. The rights of man
and of the citizen are only abstractions of the mind. They
are neither observable nor measurable. The needs of man
are concrete and lie within the realm of experience. The
role of society is to furnish each individual with the material
and mental environment capable of satisfying his basic
needs. The aim of society is to produce perfect human
beings just as the aim of each individual should be to contribute to the formation of a perfect society.

Besides natural needs, there are artificial ones whose non-
satisfaction neither injures man nor slows down his progress.
Nevertheless, every individual has an innate tendency to
satisfy certain of his real needs in an exaggerated way: for
example his need for freedom, nourishment, security or rest.
In order not to degenerate, man should only satisfy his needs
in the measure allowed by the three great laws of life.

Individuals differ in sex and age and in mental and physiological aptitudes. Some are made to think and others to act.
Others, again, have an innate gift for leadership while many
cannot govern even themselves. The observation of men
shows that two types of association exist universally. The
associations of the first type are composed of heterogeneous

but complementary elements. They resemble those of the organs in the living body. They are called organismic associations. Examples of these are the natural community formed by father, mother and children, the primitive village or the family group which works its land in common. Industrial enterprise would be greatly benefited by being transformed into an organismic association.

Associations of the second type are composed of elements which are homogeneous and noncomplementary. They can be compared with associations of similar organs, such as brains, stomachs, hearts or hands. These are called organic associations. Their type is represented by a class of children, a regiment of soldiers, a trade union or a religious community. Organic groups are only useful if they cooperate with other organic groups to form a harmonious social organism. Any organic group which develops egotistically for itself alone plays the same role in the social body as a cancer in the human body.

Members of organismic and organic groups are equal only in the sense that they are all human beings. But they are unequal in inherited potentialities and acquired aptitudes. Nevertheless, the inequality of individual capacities and social functions does not entail an inequality of worth. The stomach and the rectum are just as indispensable as the brain or the eyes. All the organs depend on the heart and the heart depends on them. The workmen are at the service of the employer just as the employer is at the service of the workmen. In an organismic community, the humblest work is no less noble than the highest. The success of a journey depends just as much on the engineer and the mechanic who made the airplane as on the expertness of the pilot.

Modern society is composed of a multitude of organismic and organic associations. Its disorder is due both to the lack of coordination of associations and institutions and to their weakness.

Every individual is a member of several organismic and organic groups. He belongs to the family, the village and the parish and also, perhaps, to a school, a trade union, a professional society or a sports club. Thus a relatively small number of completely developed individuals can have a great influence on many community groups.

If, by the transformation of a sufficiently important minority through rational discipline, a community based on similarity or solidarity could transform itself, even partially, into a community of love, its success would be certain. One can see such a success in a family where great grandparents, grandparents, parents and children form a large group of extremely heterogeneous elements which are linked together by their complementary functions and their mutual affection. It would also be possible to see it in a village whose inhabitants abstained from mutual criticism and stopped detesting each other. If only employers and workmen would decide to obey the basic laws of life, the whole character of their relations would be transformed. Industrial enterprise, instead of being a battlefield for class warfare, would become an organismic community based on solidarity and love. Its success would be assured for, if a man works badly under the influence of necessity and fear, his production increases in quality and quantity when he cooperates in an enterprise which belongs to him and to which he belongs. The success of collective life is conditioned by the social as well as the personal value of every individual.

CHAPTER SEVEN

Teaching the Laws of Conduct. Aptitude for Behaving Rationally

1	*Hereditary Inaptitude for Rational Conduct.—Types of Deficients.—Partial and Total Inaptitude.—Number of Degenerates.*

Many individuals behave badly because of defects which they bring into the world with them. Hereditary taints are often difficult to distinguish from acquired ones. The influence of the environment very often accentuates hereditary defects. In the children of alcoholics, for example, the congenital inferiority of the tissues and the mind is aggravated by the disorder, dirt, ignorance and misery of the home background. Nearly always, innate vices develop rather than diminish in the course of a lifetime. Certain features of the face and, as Galton has shown, certain qualities of mind frequently characterize a family for several generations. The same applies to feeble-mindedness and madness. Criminality, however, is only transmitted hereditarily insofar as it is linked with mental disease.

The son of a thief or a murderer is more likely to behave rationally than the son of a madman. Individuals whose behavior is congenitally vitiated are found in all classes of

177

society. Eugenism is the most neglected of all disciplines. Submen are frequently found among the descendants of alcoholics, drug-fiends and syphilitics. They also come from stock which has produced moral idiots, imbeciles and perverts. But they still occur in highly moral families, for the nervous or mental defect of an ancestor can reappear suddenly among his descendants. Before they are born, such individuals are destined to be more or less completely incapable of directing their own lives.

They belong to very different types. There are the hypersensitive who turn in on themselves before the difficulties of life, who are hurt by every obstacle or who rush into action without sufficient thought. There are the unstable whose existence is passed in starting enterprises and never finishing them; there are the dreamers, the erratic and the aboulic with their plans that never materialize; there are those whose judgment is chronically false and who are invariably wrong in their estimates of men and events. There are the lazy, immobilized in pathological inertia; the envious who, incapable of acting themselves, are content to criticize others; the moral idiots, characterized by emotional deficiencies ranging from mere clouding of the moral sense to definite perversion. There are also the host of the small-minded, the weak and the semi-invalid whom fear makes malicious. Perhaps the strange perfidy and hatred which characterize certain nations have weakness, stupidity and cowardice as their principal cause.

Many of these defects are only partially hereditary in origin. It is impossible to determine in which measure they are attributable to the structure of the tissues and the consciousness or to bad habits acquired during development. Nevertheless, we can be sure that extreme types of feeble-mindedness, mental unbalance, impulsiveness, apathy and malice are the expression of the original poor quality of soul and body.

There are many degrees in this inaptitude for rational conduct. A small part of the population can act in such a way as to be dangerous to the majority. Madmen, idiots and criminals are quite unfit to be allowed to conduct their lives freely and it is necessary to segregate them. A second category consists of those who are physically and mentally stunted: these, without being dangerous to the community, are nevertheless a burden on it. Such are the weak, the tuberculous, the unadaptable and the chronically idle.

A third category contains those who are fit to conduct their own material existence but who cause division and disorder in the community by their absence of moral sense and in particular by their habit of backbiting and scandal-mongering.

It is impossible to distinguish, among these people who are only partially incapable of behaving reasonably, those who are obeying hereditary inclinations from those who are the victims of education and environment. But both alike are more harmful to society than those whose total unfitness to conduct their own lives has caused them to be shut away.

What is the proportion of those whose ancestral defects prevent them from conforming to the rules of life? No inventory has been made of hereditary syphilitics; of the children of alcoholics; of the descendants of the feeble-minded, moral idiots or the insane.

American statistics have shown that the population contains 4 to 5 per cent of individuals susceptible to mental disturbances and 3 per cent of criminals, not counting mental defectives. This means that in every thousand persons in the United States there are at least a hundred incapable of conforming to the moral disciplines of existence. In France we have not even such very approximate statistics but we know that there are probably as many insane people as in the United States.

The majority of taints in the French people are not of ancestral origin. Probably more than half the population has an inherited patrimony good enough to permit it to behave reasonably well.

2 | *Acquired Inaptitude for Rational Conduct.—Its Causes.—Absence of Physiological and Moral Training.—Errors of Education.—Alcoholism.*

Many individuals who have a good heredity are rendered unfitted for rational behavior by other equally grave defects. These defects are due to bad conditions during the pregnancy or during the birth and development of the child. It is probable that 25 per cent of the cases of idiocy are due to stoppages or disturbances in the development of the brain which occur in the course of the fetal life, at the moment of birth or in early childhood.

In childhood and youth, any disorders which occur in the formation of the endocrine glands and the nervous system inevitably react on the consciousness. In the high valleys of the Alps, as in those of the Himalayas, absence of iodine prevents the development of the thyroid gland. As a result, the children become myxedematous cretins.

The balance of the nervous system, the acuteness and harmony of the mind largely depend on the nature of the chemical substances contained in the nourishment during the formative period of the brain and the glands. Lack of vitamins and mineral salts, insufficiency and bad quality of protein substances are probably the cause of certain intellectual and moral deficiencies.

It is obvious that the nervous system, the organs and the mind of children fed on coffee, white bread, sugar, jam and even alcohol cannot but be defective. Just as the lack of balance of phosphorus and calcium leaves the mark of rickets on the bones, so wrong diet in childhood leaves permanent traces on body and mind.

There are also physiological and mental habits which leave indelible marks on the personality. In modern society we naturally form the habit of disliking any kind of discomfort and a repugnance to any moral and physical effort except that demanded by sport. We also acquire the habit of intellectual superficiality, moral irresponsibility and verbosity. Our appetites are undisciplined; our diet is overabundant, insufficient or ill-balanced; we sleep too much or too little; we are prone to sexual excesses or perversion. A young Frenchman of good social family is usually characterized by vanity, lack of intelligence, egoism and a strange inability to grasp reality. His intelligence is narrow, sharp and abstract: he only applies it to the concrete when it is a question of his personal interest.

Men take no account of the significance of the events which are shattering civilization. They are shut up in themselves like convicts in a jail and their chances of escaping the cataclysm are extremely slight. There do exist, however, especially among older people, more alert, open-minded and educated types. In particular there are those who have an inkling of the truth, who can distinguish good from evil but who can make a stand for neither. Like those angels, neither faithful nor rebellious, whom Dante met in the first circle of hell, they remain neutral. They are, in fact, morally atrophied and as such belong to the class of submen.

| 3 | *Aptitude for Rational Conduct.—Rarity of* Homo Sapiens. |

In the midst of the vast flock of the degenerate, the corrupt and the foolish, there are still many people capable of behaving reasonably. These include all children with a good heredity, adults who have remained healthy and, above all, those of ripe age who have kept the freshness and plasticity of youth. An important minority of the population, in towns as well as in the country, has preserved the traditional habits of honor, morality and courage. Even in contaminated and more or less degenerate families, there are still some normal individuals. It is probable that the present decadence is not incurable, for it results from the wilting of the individual under the influence of the environment rather than from a lesion of the germ plasma. In other words, it is not the outcome of racial degeneration. Although our civilization is in very great danger, it is not in anything like the desperate state of Roman civilization during the first centuries of the Christian era.

At that time the line of empire builders was rapidly dying out and being replaced by that of their slaves. The decadence of the moderns, on the contrary, is mainly due to their habits of life and thought. There are, of course, in France, as in New England, sections of the population which seem to be really degenerate. It does not look as if good hereditary qualities will ever revive in certain Breton villages which are undermined by consanguinity, alcoholism, tuberculosis and cancer. But there remains sufficient good stock for regeneration to be possible.

In the dawn of their lives young human beings grow, as

joyfully as young animals, according to the laws of nature. They slip spontaneously into reality. If they are not spoiled by their family or their school, they are enthusiastic, eager to love and willing to sacrifice themselves for an ideal. Heroism comes naturally to them. They readily adopt new habits and they are not afraid of the truth. Nothing prevents them from submitting to the eternal disciplines of life. This is why it is not in the least Utopian to undertake the transformation of the attitude of the entire youth of a country toward fundamental human problems.

What at this moment is the proportion of individuals who deserve the name of *homo sapiens?* It is impossible to collect statistics of people whose conduct is rational. We possess no sure test of character, judgment, nervous equilibrity, moral sense and robustness of spirit. It is very useful to be able to measure psychological age for thus we can detect the weak-minded who are incapable of reasonable behavior. On the other hand, neither a high intelligence quotient nor success in difficult examinations is any proof of wisdom.

It is said that, if only a few hundred people were suddenly kidnaped in New York, the whole city would be entirely paralyzed. The number of men capable of governing themselves and others is certainly extremely small; so small that wisdom seems to have disappeared from the face of the earth.

But may not this perhaps be an illusion? Was the world wiser formerly than it is today? Are there fewer individuals capable of guiding themselves at the present time than there were in classical civilization, the Middle Ages or the eighteenth century?

Periods of decadence are probably distinguished from others by the high proportion of human failures. The elite is then stifled by the mass of the weak and the defective.

Perhaps certain periods of history are characterized by

the brief flowering of a humanity really fitted for self-guid-
ance. Such epochs may have occurred in the time of Pericles,
at the moment of the foundation of Rome or in the great age
of the cathedrals. Possibly Thomas Jefferson would not have
written the Declaration of Independence if he had not
judged the Americans worthy of liberty. Like the animals,
homo sapiens has retreated before the advance of civilization.

4 | *How to Prepare Man to Receive Instruction in Ra-
tional Conduct.*

The rules of reasonable behavior will remain empty for-
mulæ if man is not rendered capable of putting these rules
into practice. It would be useless to teach things which no
one can learn except children and a negligible number of
adults. We moderns are ill-fitted to conduct ourselves rationally; hereditary and acquired defects prevent us from
understanding and applying the rules. The very future of
the white race is seriously threatened. Let us hope that the
Western nations will realize how rapidly the evil is gaining
ground before it becomes incurable. How can man be prepared to receive instruction in the laws of behavior? How
can each person be given the anatomical and mental substratum indispensable to building up his personality?

CHAPTER EIGHT

Teaching the Laws of Life

Particular Character of This Teaching.—Necessity for Example.

It would be easy to propound the laws of conduct and their scientific base in a series of didactic lessons as one teaches geography or grammar. Any good teacher could accomplish this task. But quite a different method is needed to train children to put these rules into practice. One does not learn to pilot an airplane by taking a course in aerodynamics. Only practice will develop the reflexes which, in all circumstances, will automatically switch us onto the right course. To be perfect, obedience to the laws of conduct should be instinctive. Anyone who has been conditioned from infancy regarding good and evil will experience no difficulty in choosing good and avoiding evil throughout his whole life. He will recoil from evil as naturally as he recoils from fire. Lying and treachery will seem to him not merely forbidden but impossible. If such reactions are to be developed in the individual, there must be an environment where moral precepts are strictly and unremittingly observed. Only example will effectively inculcate the rules of life. Man, like the monkey, has an innate tendency to imitate but he imitates evil more easily than good. The child unconsciously models himself on his companions, teachers and parents; above all, on the movie heroes and the real or imaginary people he reads about. Fénelon said that this imitative tendency in children produces endless evils when they are left to unprincipled people who do not control themselves in their presence. People can only teach things in which they believe and children are never deceived by hypocrisy. To teach others to behave well, one must first of all behave well oneself.

For this reason the technology of existence demands an appropriate milieu, a social group where intellectual, physiological and moral rules are habitually put into practice. Neither the family nor the school has been capable of satisfactorily furnishing this milieu. Today French schools have reduced education to a kind of thin intellectual veneer. The nonintellectual activities of the spirit, particularly the moral sense and the sense of beauty, are unknown to the majority of teachers. The immense effort of the New Education is mainly directed toward the intellectual and social facets of the personality. In the Montessori schools, in those run according to the principles of John Dewey and Decroly and those where the Dalton Plan is applied, there are coordinated processes for developing the individuality of children of all ages. Nevertheless, the majority of these children remain incapable of playing their natural part in society. It is strange that the young people who are today looking on so passively while civilization crumbles are the products of the "active" school. They have proved to be ill-educated, sly, dishonest and lacking in character and moral sense. May not these defects be due to some serious gap in their teaching? How many pedagogues, for example, address themselves to training the will and encouraging self-mastery?

Generally speaking, the family is a deplorable educational

milieu, for modern parents know nothing about the psychology of childhood and youth. They are too naïve, too neurotic, too weak or too stern. One could almost say that the majority of them cultivate the art of producing defects in their children. They are occupied, above all, with their own work and their own pleasures. Too many children witness bad manners, quarrels, selfishness and even drunkenness in their own families. If they are not initiated into such aspects of life by their parents, they will inevitably be so initiated by their companions.

To sum up, neither the school nor the family is capable nowadays of teaching the young how to behave. Consequently, modern youth reflects the mediocrity of its educators like a mirror. Education which limits itself to preparation for examinations, to a mere exercise of memory instead of forming the mind produces only "donkeys loaded with books." Young people brought up in this way are incapable of understanding reality and of playing their natural part in society.

2 | *Building Up an Educational Milieu.—Schools for Parents and Teachers.*

In our present state of moral disorder it would be an arduous enterprise to build up the right kind of educational milieu for the moral training we have seen to be so highly necessary. We have discussed earlier the possibility of forming small groups which could escape the bad influences of modern society by submitting themselves to a rule similar to military or monastic discipline. Such associations should be formed by those who have abandoned the sentimental fictions of Rousseau, the pseudo-science of Durckheim and

Dewey, the dogmas of Liberalism and modern amoralism and who wish to substitute rational principles of behavior for these fantasies. States would then be able to depend on such associations for the establishing of a suitable educational environment. Only the government has the necessary authority to help the successful direction of educational work. To adapt the social milieu to the necessities of education demands first of all a vast spring-cleaning. There must be effective censorship of the movies and the radio. The majority of dance halls, cabarets and bars should be closed. The periodical literature which our children and young people so eagerly devour needs to be radically transformed. Once this purifying process has been accomplished, it will be necessary to proceed to the education of parents and teachers. Parents and teachers are generally full of good will and err mainly through ignorance. From now onwards we ought to give future parents and teachers the knowledge they lack concerning the conduct of their own lives and the education of children. It is far easier to rear chickens and lambs than to bring up small human beings. Yet anyone who wants to go in for breeding animals is apprenticed on a farm or in an agricultural college. No one would be so foolish as to prepare themselves for this work by studying literature, mathematics or philosophy yet this is the very folly which young girls commit today. The majority of them know practically nothing outside their school curriculum.

They come to marriage totally ignorant of their tasks as women. It is obvious that there should be special schools where young girls would learn the facts of life and how to train their children. Such an education would take several years and would in no way resemble the teaching given in domestic science schools or child-welfare centers. What is needed is a harmonious training of all the feminine functions, physical as well as mental. These functions are just as important as the masculine ones but their character is entirely different. To give the same education to boys and girls is a superannuated notion; a survival of the prescientific era of human history.

At the time of the Renaissance men had a deeper and juster view of education than our twentieth century pedagogues. Erasmus thought that a woman should be educated for herself, for her husband and for her children. Her duty is not merely to suckle her offspring but to give them their first education and to make them fit to govern themselves. All young girls and young mothers ought to be initiated into the methods of harmoniously developing the whole of a child's mental and organic activities.

3 | *Integral Formation of the Individual.*

Integral formation consists in developing to the highest degree all the hereditary potentialities. Education is, therefore, very much more than the methodical socialization of the young generation as Durckheim believed. Actually it consists in the gentle, tenacious and powerful action of the educator on the feelings, intelligence and body of his pupil.

We know that, during growth, the body can be modeled by five groups of factors. Firstly, by physical factors such as heat, cold, wind, rain and the variations of these factors. Secondly, by chemical factors contained in food and drink. Thirdly, by physiological factors which consist principally in the discipline of alimentation, intestinal evacuation, sleep, muscular and organic activities and also in the unconscious effort of the adaptive systems and in the conscious effort of manual work and games. Fourthly, come the intellectual factors by which the child learns how to learn. In other words he learns how to look, how to remember, how to judge, how to make contact with reality. Fifthly, there are the moral factors or habits of conduct. The most important of the latter are training of the will, self-control, cleanliness, truthfulness, courage and the ability to distinguish sharply between good and evil. The educator must never limit himself to using only one of these groups of factors. It is also necessary that these agencies should be daily employed in forming a child from the earliest possible moment, in fact from the day after its birth. This is why it is far more necessary for a mother than for a teacher to know the existence of the mechanisms of development and the way to utilize them.

Any healthy child easily learns the physiological, mental and social rules proper to its age. Apprenticeship to life is at first purely training. But it is the training of little creatures capable of listening to reason and liking to be treated as reasonable beings. One must use arguments appropriate to the child's mind. A child easily understands that such and such an act displeases its parents. It is, like a little dog, sensitive to the praise or blame of those it loves.

If it has a good heredity, it is easily led by feeling. But, as it has no judgment, it should be strictly subjected to its parents' will. The teaching of the laws of life is, at the beginning, entirely practical. It consists, first, in the child's experimental verification of the line which separates the permissible from the forbidden; then, in the implanting of the idea of good and evil. It is only later that it can be initiated into the idea of law and the duty of thinking and acting in daily life according to absolute and unchangeable principles.

But, long before the reason is sufficiently developed to grasp the rational basis of the rules of conduct, physiological and mental formation should already be well advanced. It is in earliest infancy that sight, hearing, smell and taste should be educated.

This is the time, too, when manual skill and nervous stability should be developed. Young children should be taught to control their excitability, to develop their will power and their capacity for effort. As Erasmus wrote, we learn everything willingly from those we love. Those who are experienced in training young animals as well as in training young children, know the profound truth of this observation. As Fénelon wisely taught, pleasure is the most important element in training a child.

Human beings, whatever their age, are far more powerfully moved by feeling than by reason. They submit themselves far more readily to the hard laws of life if these appear to them as the will of God instead of the expression of some blind force. They are more willing to obey a person than a principle. The impassible God of Aristotle leaves them indifferent but they tend to love a God who is personally interested in them. Particularly is this true if this God did not disdain, only two thousand years ago, to manifest Himself on earth in a body like their own. Thus religious teaching in general and particularly that of the Christian *mystique* has immense educational value.

It is, of course, a waste of time to talk to children of theology and duty. But we should follow Kant's advice and present God to them very early indeed as an invisible father who watches over them and to whom they can address prayers. The true mode of honoring God consists in fulfilling His will. And the will of God is undoubtedly that the child, like the man, should behave reasonably.

The esthetic sense is very close to the religious; beauty has a great educative power. When it takes the form of sacrifice, heroism and holiness it irresistibly attracts men toward the heights. It is this beauty which gives life its meaning, nobility and joy. We must show every child that any existence, however humble and painful it may be, becomes radiant when it is illuminated by an ideal of beauty and love.

4 | *Renovation of Schools.—Masters of Integral Educa-tion and the Conduct of Life.*

We are now faced with the problem of the complete renovation of our educational system. The failure of modern education is due partly to parents shirking their responsibilities and partly to the preeminence given by pedagogues to intellectual studies. Certainly this emphasis on intellectual culture is quite justified for we need all forms of knowledge. But we should further intellectual progress, not by overloading the school programs but by improving the techniques of teaching. On the other hand, the events of these last years have demonstrated the individual and social insufficiency of the young people turned out by our schools and universities. What is the use of developing science, letters, art and philosophy if society is disintegrating?

If our civilization is to survive, we must all be prepared to live, not according to ideologies, but according to the order of things. We therefore need to substitute integral education for the exclusively intellectual type on which we have hitherto concentrated. We need to actualize all the hereditary potentialities of the individual and to set the individual thus formed in the framework of cosmic and social reality.

But we possess no teachers of integral education. We must begin, therefore, by organizing schools for the training of such teachers; schools where the principles, rules and technique of rational conduct would be taught. These schools would also serve as research centers for human typology, physiology, psychology and the elaboration of new methods of teaching.

These specially trained masters would have a double mission. Some would teach schoolmasters the ideas of integral education which they have hitherto lacked. Others would be responsible for giving pupils in schools and universities the physiological and spiritual training which has been totally neglected.

It is important to give neither spiritual nor physiological training the supremacy hitherto accorded to the intellectual. The task of the professor of integral education in every school will be to build up complete human beings. He will first have to discover the capabilities of the pupils by appropriate tests and classify them according to the data of biotypology; then he will have to develop in each one, as completely as the pupils' inherited predispositions permit, self-control and the other qualities we have mentioned. At the same time, he will keep in constant touch with doctors; with his colleagues in the physical, intellectual and artistic fields; with the priests responsible for religious education and with the parents. Thus he will be able to coordinate these very diverse influences with the aim of making each child a harmoniously balanced person. He will, in fact, be the real head of the school.

No one denies that we need great specialists, scientists, engineers, doctors, artists and economists. The aim of integral education is to prevent a man from becoming dehumanized even if he has to spend his life in a laboratory, a library, a factory, an office or a hospital.

CHAPTER NINE

The Success of Life

1 | *General Considerations.*

Through its own fault, civilized humanity has brought an immense catastrophe upon itself. War resolves none of the fundamental human problems; all that it does is to establish the supremacy of one nation over others. In the chaos which follows the end of hostilities, these problems pose themselves afresh. It is only on ourselves that we can count for their solution.

Our future depends on our aptitude to behave ourselves rationally. It depends, above all, on our will to follow the rules of our existence strictly. The crisis of humanity is the result of its absurd conduct. Hitherto, no society has conducted itself in a natural fashion for spirit has not been capable of replacing instinct.

No civilization has succeeded in giving man rules of conduct completely conformed to his structure and an environment perfectly adapted to it. The Roman Empire crumbled; the splendor of the age of the cathedrals has vanished and we are assisting at the death agony of the society which began so hopefully with the Declaration of Independence and the French Revolution. At the dawn of that society, liberty, the reign of science and the industrial revolution seemed as if they must give unlimited happiness to the human race.

The fact is that human life is not a success. One might say that it has run into an impasse as at the time when creative evolution produced the dinosaurs, those gigantic beasts with small heads who were incapable of adapting themselves. The intellect, divorced from feeling by its egotistical development, is a monstrosity which seems as if it may render man incapable of surviving. This is the disruption of life, the war which destroys the fittest. The means of destruction are progressing faster than the means of helping life. We have arrived at this singular moment of human history where we must either succeed or sink to our ruin in chaos and degeneration.

The capital task of humanity is not production, art or science but the ensuring of the success of life itself. Humanity must realize that its fate lies in its own hands. An entirely new enterprise and a gigantic effort are now imposed on the world's inhabitants, an undertaking which should absorb the energy of all nations. What we have to do is nothing less than to reset the course of evolution toward a higher life. Now that man has substituted his own intelligence and will for the mystery of evolutionary forces, we must either rise higher or perish.

We can at least begin to distinguish through the mists of dawn the road which leads to our salvation. But how many of the mass of civilized people are capable of even perceiving this road? How many will have the courage to set out on it by an immediate personal effort; by a revolutionary change in their way of thinking, acting and behaving toward others which will only come about through self-mastery?

Civilization is first and foremost a discipline; a discipline which is physiological, moral and scientific. Barbarism, on the contrary, is essentially undisciplined. But whereas primitive barbarism was subject to the harsh authority of nature, our anemic modern barbarism is completely unrestrained.

The task which confronts us today is to take up the march of humanity at the point where, four hundred years ago, it strayed into an impasse and became engulfed in the material. In the new city, the spiritual and the material should be inseparable, although ruled by different laws. The rule of the road is the same for believers and unbelievers; the former think that the rules come from God Himself, the latter that they come from nature. Prayer gives believers an advantage over the rest. The only means of curing ourselves is to follow the laws of life.

By transforming ourselves we should become capable, even in the midst of suffering and disaster, of gradually transforming our environment and our institutions. Then at last we might be able to use the power of science to develop the inherited potentialities of our race in the best possible way and to build up, on the ruins of modern society, a world modeled on the true needs of human beings.

2 | *How to Ensure Success.*

We must not imagine that we can behave according to the whims either of our spirit or our senses. Neither must we be guided by the partial truths of religions or philosophical systems. By his instinct of self-interest, by revelation and also by the free play of his intelligence man has learned how to guide himself, but only in a limited way. He has achieved a partial ascent but, at intervals, he has gone astray and whole nations have fallen into the abyss.

None of his attempts have fully succeeded. Classical civilization, the Middle Ages, Liberalism, Marxism and National Socialism have all failed.

Philosophical principles are, and always will be, incomplete since they only express the prejudices of one man. Materialism and idealism are equally false; hence their downfall. Whoever leans entirely on the spiritual, the intellectual or the material is equally doomed to failure. Separately, the priest, the teacher and the doctor are incapable of ensuring the success of life; they can only do so by pooling their knowledge.

The success of life is compatible with many faults and errors. But lying, duplicity, apathy and inactivity are completely opposed to it. In primitive life inactivity and weakness are always punished by death. Lying and treachery are of human invention. Dante places traitors in the deepest abyss of hell, in the well of ice where Satan himself resides.

Liberalism and Marxism have not been able to give men the conditions necessary to the development of life.

Liberalism is designed for the property-owning classes. It lacks that passionate element which alone drives men to action. It offers a narrow philosophy and meager abstractions of reality. It has distorted the spirit and, because of this, it has not succeeded. The Liberal Bourgeois is the elder brother of the Bolshevist.

Marxism does possess the passionate element and the ideal of the liberation of the oppressed but it is based on a philosophical doctrine. It has saints and martyrs; it has a titanic grandeur. In Marxism, passion engenders resentment; the battle of the dispossessed against the possessors, the oppression of the rich by the poor.

The break-up of Western civilization is due to the failure of ideologies, to the insufficiency both of religion and science. If life is to triumph, we need a revolution. We must re-examine every question and make an act of faith in the power of the human spirit. Our destiny demands this great effort; we ought to devote all our time to the effort of living since this is the whole purpose of our being on earth.

All men who are determined to make a success of living in the widest sense should join together as they have done in all times. Pythagoras made the first attempt, but it is the Catholic Church which has hitherto offered the most complete of such associations. We must give up the illusion that we can live according to instinct, like the bees. True, the success of life demands, above all, an effort of intelligence and will. Since intelligence has not replaced instinct we must try to render it capable of directing life.

None of the acquisitions made by humanity must be set aside. By utilizing at the same time intellect and faith, science and religion, mathematics and love, we shall be able to do what science and religion, acting separately, have been incapable of doing.

The road to the triumph of life is a royal road. It does not consist in the search for happiness. Man is so constructed that, consciously or not, he spends his life seeking it. Yet this pursuit has always been fruitless. The moralities of pleasure and utilitarianism have not kept their promises.

Happiness cannot be attained directly nor is it what we usually imagine it to be. The only happiness man can attain is that which results from the perfect functioning of body and soul and from the accomplishment of the destiny which the order of things assigns to him.

The only means, therefore, of attaining happiness is to aim at the widest possible fulfillment of life. It is useless to pursue happiness as an end in itself; when life succeeds as a whole, happiness appears as a by-product.

Let us begin by changing ourselves, something which each one of us is capable of doing. Then we shall all be on the same road and we shall all contribute to the common strength and the common joy.

*

3 | *Success of Collective Life.*

For many people, all that is needed is to extend their range. Thus the mystics ought to fulfill themselves also on the physiological and intellectual side. The same applies to the Liberal intellectuals and to those whose ideal is the freeing of the oppressed. Each needs to develop the sides of his personality which he has neglected.

Collective life has not the same rules of conduct as individual life, just as the morality of individuals and the morality of nations are not identical. Community life has never succeeded except during short periods. Yet it is, nevertheless, possible, even if a society contains many antisocial individuals. But its rules must be based not on philosophical concepts but on scientific ones. Since the structure of the community necessarily derives from that of individuals, scientific knowledge of individuals and their reciprocal relations ought to be the foundation of the social organization. Both Liberalism and Marxism, based alike on philosophical ideas, give a too exclusive importance to economics. But humanity is more important than economics.

Man is *homo faber* because he is *homo sapiens*. His skill in working depends on the perfect coordination between brain and hand.

Communities and industrial enterprises should be conceived as organisms whose function is to build up centers of human brotherhood where all are equal in the sense in which the Church understands men's equality; that is to say, in the sense that all are children of God.

There will always be biological inequalities, inequalities of physique, sex, vitality, intelligence and aptitude. In an organismic community, individuals are like the organs of the body, unequal in structure and potentialities but equal in that all are essential for the perfection of the brain and the soul. Social classes are thus irrelevant.

Social classes emerged originally from biological superiority. They have become odious because they have persisted after this superiority has disappeared and, most of all, because those who belong to the upper classes have exaggerated their superiority and been unwilling to recognize the nobility which exists in the lower. If biological classes cannot be suppressed, we can at least give to all the possibility of bettering their life and developing their spirit. They must be given the chance of developing feeling as well as intelligence.

Biological inequality entails inequality of earning; difference of work involves difference of life. Thus in a theatrical company, there is a difference between the actors, and when children play at coaches, one is the coachman and the other the horses.

The suppression of the Proletariat and the liberation of the oppressed should not come about through class warfare but through the abolition of social classes.

What is needed is to suppress the Proletariat by replacing it with industrial enterprise of an organismic character. If the community has an organismic character, it matters little whether the state or private individuals own the means of production, but individual ownership of house and land is indispensable.

4 | *Setting the Religious Sense to Work.—Christianity.*

The success of life implies the full accomplishment of our spiritual destiny, whatever it may be.

The religious sense, like the esthetic, is a fundamental physiological activity; it is in no sense the consequence of an unsatisfactory economic state. We need to use all the present forms of life. The most effective is the Christian form in the mystical sense which advocates union with God and with other human beings. The Catholic Church is the most complete expression of this.

Why have the white races not succeeded in spite of their Christianity? What is the reason for the present chaos? Why did the society of the Middle Ages end in failure? Why did Christianity, which has such clear-cut intuitions of human nature, not continue its ascent after the Middle Ages?

Christianity offers men the very highest of moralities; one very close to that indicated by our structure. It presents to them a God who can be adored because He is within our reach and Whom we ought to love. It has inspired martyrs; it has always respected life, the race and the spirit. But it has not brought peace to the world. What is the reason for this lack of success?

It thoroughly understands the laws of mysticism but not the laws of life. Christian inspiration has not been incorporated in rational forms of life. It has neglected physiology for the intellect. By tolerating social classes, the oppression of the poor by the rich, the dispossession of one class of men, it has been incorporated into types of community which are not viable.

We must render to God the things which are God's and to

Caesar the things which are Caesar's. The Church cannot substitute itself for Caesar nor confuse itself with him. Caesar and the Church are opposed to each other in the same way that feeling, reason and the organs are opposed in a human being.

It would be easy to give Christianity and even Catholicism what they lack—the added balance of physical knowledge. Thus we should be able to prevent the physiological or intellectual degeneration which inevitably entails moral decadence. Christian inspiration must be incorporated in social forms created, not according to philosophical principles, but after the pattern of the structure of life.

5 | *The Future.*

To prepare the society of tomorrow, we must first grasp the reality of today. This apprehension of reality demands a sincere and persistent effort to understand the events going on about us, not only in our own village or town but also in the nation and the world.

No effort is more difficult. Both in Europe and in America we are all alike immersed in the lies of the radio as well as those of newspapers and books. The subtle techniques of propaganda have to all intents and purposes suppressed liberty of thought. We have not fully realized the humiliation and danger of this new form of slavery and we have not yet learned how to rebel against it.

Furthermore, during catastrophic periods of history, a strange darkness always spreads over the masses as well as over their leaders. The French, for example, have not yet understood the significance of the defeat. They continue to

live obstinately with the ghosts of the past in a world as unreal as a stage setting.

The democracies of Europe and America suffer from a
declining birth rate, from diminished public and private
wealth and from an enormous increase of expenditure due
to the war. The same symptoms were observable during the
Peloponnesian War at the beginning of the decline of ancient
Greece. But, just as in Greece, the causes of our decline are
moral rather than political or economic. In the years before
the war, the disunity and lack of patriotism of the people
and the dishonesty of their leaders were no less evident in
France than in Greece at the time of Demosthenes.

It is important to understand that the principal phenomenon of our time is not universal war. Undoubtedly the last
war was a formidable event in the history of Europe. It was,
nevertheless, only an accident; a sharp crisis in a chronic
disease, hitherto incurable, which has attacked all former
civilizations at a certain point in their history.

The danger is, therefore, extreme. Nevertheless, we have
some reason to hope that history will not repeat itself for us
since we possess means of knowing and acting not available
to our ancestors. For the first time in the history of the
world, a civilization which has arrived at the verge of its
decline is able to diagnose its ills. Perhaps it will be able
to use this knowledge and, thanks to the marvelous forces
of science, to avoid the common fate of all the great peoples
of the past. We ought to launch ourselves on this new path
from this very moment.

We are incapable, in our present state of division and confusion, of transforming our institutions all at once. Modern
society is a heavy construction weighed down with all the
errors of the past. At this moment we have neither the intelligence nor the strength to build up every single part of
a new world. Before renewing our institutions, we must reno-

vate ourselves and this effort of renovation can be begun here and now by anyone who chooses. It may seem absurd to believe that we, obscure as we are, should be capable of effecting the revival of our nation by a tiny individual effort. Yet a very feeble effort becomes irresistible when it is multiplied millions of times. No one should think his contribution to the common work useless, however insignificant it may seem to himself.

Nothing is harder than to strip oneself of one's egoism, intemperance, boorishness and laziness; of all those vices which arrest the development of our personality and make us odious to others.

We must go untiringly repeating this extremely arduous and difficult attempt to reconstruct ourselves, with the help of physiology and psychology, until we succeed. Once we have recovered our strength and our clearness of vision, we can begin the transformation of our methods of education, our ways of life, our legislation and our government. Thus, little by little, there will develop a social environment in which the generation which succeeds us will be able to develop all the potentialities hidden in the germ plasm. It is thus that, stone by stone, the new City will come to be built.

Life only develops to its fullest and best in appropriate conditions, conditions which society has gradually created over thousands of years. Isolated and independent man has never existed except in the imagination of Jean-Jacques Rousseau. We depend entirely on other men: on those who live with us and above all on those who have preceded us. Society is composed of the dead as well as the living. Robinson Crusoe would not have survived without the help of the tools and the weapons he found. Even in his solitude, he benefited from the efforts of other men.

The future will be what we are ourselves. It is beyond doubt that the principle of least effort, the morality of pleas-

ure and Liberalism are in contradiction to the laws of conduct inscribed in the very structure of our body and soul.
They must therefore be firmly rejected.

What will life, as it demands to be lived, give us in ex-
change for the satisfaction of our sloth and our appetites?
At first it will bring us effort, sacrifice and suffering like any
discipline intended for the training of the mind, organs or
muscles. Later it will bring us something of inestimable
value; something of which those who live only for pleasure,
profit or amusement will always be deprived. This peculiar,
indefinable joy, which one must have felt oneself to understand, is the sign with which life marks its moment of
triumph; the moment when our physical and mental activities
attain the end prescribed by the order of things. It is the
joy of the runner breasting the tape, of the artist before his
work, of the woman hearing the first cry of her newborn
child, of the scientist on the verge of a discovery, of the hero
leading his people to victory, of the saint falling asleep in
the peace of the Lord.

Before those who perfectly perform their task as men, the
road of truth lies always open. On this royal road, the poor
as well as the rich, the weak as well as the strong, believer
and unbeliever alike are invited to advance. If they accept
this invitation, they are sure of accomplishing their destiny,
of participating in the sublime work of evolution, of hasten-
ing the coming of the Kingdom of God on earth. And, over
and above, they will attain all the happiness compatible with
our human condition.

THE AUTHOR AND HIS BOOK

ALEXIS CARREL, surgeon, biologist and author, was born in Ste. Foy-les-Lyon, France, on June 28, 1873; he died in Paris on November 5, 1944. In those eventful seventy-one years, his wide variety of interests brought him many opportunities for fame. In 1912, while on the staff of the Rockefeller Institute in New York City, he was awarded the Nobel Prize for his success in suturing blood vessels and transplanting organs. Returning to France to join the French Army in World War I, he there perfected, with Henry D. Dakin, the Carrel-Dakin solution for the treatment of infected wounds. And, in 1934, working with Charles A. Lindbergh, he developed an "artificial heart" for use in scientific experimentation. His first popular book was Man the Unknown (Harper, 1935), one of the great bestsellers of modern times, which brought him to the attention of a broader public. When World War II broke out, he once again returned from America to his native France to serve in his country's hour of need. After the German occupation, he was appointed by the Vichy government to head the French Foundation for the Study of Human Problems and held that post until the liberation of France. Embittered by criticism of his wartime activities, he died only two weeks after the De Gaulle government had cleared him of charges of collaboration. Since his death, two books prior to this work have been published in the United States: Prayer (Morehouse-Gorham, 1948) and The Voyage to Lourdes (Harper, 1950).

REFLECTIONS ON LIFE (Hawthorn, 1953) was designed by Sidney Feinberg and completely manufactured by American Book–Stratford Press, Inc. The body type is Caledonia, designed for the Linotype by W. A. Dwiggins, one of America's best-known typographers and designers. The paper is an antique finish stock manufactured by the S. D. Warren Company.

A HAWTHORN BOOK

CPSIA information can be obtained
at www.ICGtesting.com
Printed in the USA
LVHW081631090323
741299LV00004B/74